Doctrinal Sermons
on the *Catechism of the Catholic Church*

T0345935

Other Titles of Interest from St. Augustine's Press

Servais Pinckaers, O.P., *Morality: The Catholic View*

C.S. Lewis & St. Giovanni Calabria, *The Latin Letters of C.S. Lewis*

James V. Schall, *The Modern Age*

James V. Schall, *The Regensburg Lecture*

James V. Schall, *Sum Total of Human Happiness*

Josef Pieper, *The Silence of St. Thomas*

Josef Pieper, *Scholasticism*

Josef Pieper, *Happiness and Contemplation*

Josef Pieper and Heinz Raskop, *What Catholics Belief*

Edward Feser, *The Last Superstition: A Refutation of the New Atheism*

Thomas Aquinas, *Commentary on the Epistle to the Hebrews*

Thomas Aquinas, *Commentaries on St. Paul's Epistles to Timothy, Titus, and Philemon*

Thomas Aquinas, *Treatise on Law: The Complete Text*

Thomas Aquinas, *Treatise on Human Nature: The Complete Text*

John of St. Thomas, *An Introduction to the Summa Theologiae of Thomas Aquinas*

St. Augustine, *On Order [De Ordine]*

St. Augustine, *The St. Augustine LifeGuide*

Karol Wojtyła, *Man in the Field of Responsibility*

John Paul II, *The John Paul II LifeGuide*

John Beaumont, *Roads to Rome: A Guide to Notable Converts from Britain and Ireland from the Reformation to the Present Day*

Gabriel Marcel, *The Mystery of Being* (2 vols.)

Gabriel Marcel, *A Gabriel Marcel Reader*

Gabriel Marcel, *Thou Shall Not Die*

Gabriel Marcel, *Man against Mass Society*

Gabriel Marcel, *Homo Viator*

Jacques Maritain, *Natural Law: Reflections on Theory and Practice*

Charles Card'l Journey, *The Mass: Presence of the Sacrifice of the Cross*

Peter Kreeft, *Summa Philosophica*

Peter Kreeft, *The Philosophy of Jesus*

Peter Kreeft, *Jesus-Shock*

Doctrinal Sermons
on the *Catechism of the Catholic Church*

Kenneth Baker, S.J.

ST. AUGUSTINE'S PRESS
South Bend, Indiana

Copyright © 2012 by Kenneth Baker, S.J.

All rights reserved. No part of this book may be reproduced, stored
in a retrieval system, or transmitted, in any form or by any means,
electronic, mechanical, photocopying, recording, or otherwise,
without the prior permission of St. Augustine's Press.

Manufactured in the United States of America

1 2 3 4 5 6   17 16 15 14 13 12

Library of Congress Cataloging in Publication Data
Baker, Kenneth, S.J.
Doctrinal sermons on the catechism of the Catholic Church /
Kenneth Baker.
p. cm.
Includes bibliographical references (p.   ).
ISBN 978-1-58731-189-5 (paperbound: alk. paper) 1. Catholic
Church. Catechismus Ecclesiae Catholicae--Sermons. 2. Catholic
Church – Catechisms –Sermons. 3. Catholic Church – Doctrines –
Sermons. I. Title.
BX1959.5.B35 2012
238'.2 – dc23   2011039530

∞ The paper used in this publication meets the minimum requirements of
the American National Standard for Information Sciences – Permanence of
Paper for Printed Materials, ANSI Z39.48-1984.

ST. AUGUSTINE'S PRESS
www.staugustine.net

CONTENTS

Introduction vii

The Bible 1
Revelation 5
Faith 9
Hope 13
Charity 16
Creed: Article 1 20
Creed: Article 2 24
Creed: Article 3 27
Creed: Article 4 30
Creed: Article 5 34
Creed: Article 6 38
Creed: Article 7 41
Creed: Article 8 45
Creed: Article 9 51
Creed: Article 10 58
Creed: Article 11 61
Creed: Article 12 64
Sacrament 1: Baptism 68
Sacrament 2: Confirmation 72
Sacrament 3: Holy Eucharist 75
Sacrament 4: Penance 79
Sacrament 5: Anointing of the Sick 83
Sacrament 6: Holy Orders 86
Sacrament 7: Matrimony 90
Commandment 1: One God 94
Commandment 2: God's Name 100
Commandment 3: Sunday 104
Commandment 4: Honor Parents 108
Commandment 5: Human Life 112
Commandment 6: No Adultery 116

Commandment 7: Stealing 121
Commandment 8: No Lying..125
Commandments 9 & 10: Coveting...129
Prudence 133
Justice 137
Temperance..141
Fortitude 145
Death 149
The Last Judgment 152
Heaven..156
Hell...160
Purgatory 164
Sin...168
Eternity 176
The Seven Gifts of the Holy Spirit: Sails of the Soul 180
The Twelve Fruits of the Holy Spirit 184
Our Father 187
Our Father 1 – Thy Name...191
Our Father 2 – Thy Kingdom..194
Our Father 3 – ThyWill Be Done 198
Our Father 4 – Daily Bread 202
Our Father 5 – Forgiveness 206
Our Father 6 – Temptation 209
Our Father 7 – Evil 213

Bibliography 216

INTRODUCTION

One of the main tasks of the Catholic priest is to preach the word of God, especially in conjunction with the readings during the celebration of Mass. There are many homily helps based on those readings which explain each phrase or idea contained in the readings from the Bible. Since Vatican II there has been much good preaching based on Holy Scripture, but there has not been a corresponding emphasis on Catholic doctrine and morals. Homilies or sermons on these subjects can be based on other parts of the Mass, such as the Gloria, the Creed and the Our Father.

Many Catholics, therefore, at this time after the Vatican Council do not have a firm grasp of many of the fundamentals of the faith. Several reasons have been adduced for this fact. It has been blamed on the power and omnipresence of the media, on the failure of catechetics, on poor sermons or homilies at the Sunday Mass, on the religious instruction in our schools and colleges. I am not sure what the precise reason is, but the fact is undeniable that on key points of doctrine and morals—such as, for example, the divinity of Christ, the Mass as a sacrifice, the evils of contraception and abortion—millions of Catholics do not know what their Church teaches. Other millions do know what she teaches, but they do not know or understand the reasons for that Church teaching. Consequently, many individuals who call themselves Catholic dissent from essential teachings of the Church, such as the Real Presence of Jesus in the Blessed Sacrament.

Briefly, what it comes down to is that millions of Catholics do not know their catechism. That is not a healthy situation for the Catholic Church. Perhaps that is a reason for the defection of about thirty million Catholics, for according to a recent Pew survey one out of every ten Americans today is an ex-Catholic.

The 54 sermons in this little volume are an attempt to remedy this situation. They cover the essentials of the faith following the outline in the *Catechism of the Catholic Church* and the

Catechism of the Council of Trent. So the sermons cover the four parts of the catechism: Apostles' Creed, Seven Sacraments, Ten Commandments, and prayer as found in the "Our Father." To put it briefly: the sermons cover Creed, Cult, Code and prayer.

Most of the sermons are not long. They average about 1,250 words each and can be given in ten to 15 minutes, depending on how much additional information is added to them by the priest who uses them. Of course, the intention is not that they should be given word for word. They offer the basic information that the preacher can organize and develop in his own way, using his own concrete examples.

These sermons can be given over the period of about one year as a series. It might be helpful to announce in the church bulletin the topic for the day and also the topic to be covered the following Sunday. If the faithful know what the topic of the next sermon is going to be, perhaps some of them will be motivated to look it up in the Catechism and read that section in advance. The preacher himself would do well to consult the pertinent part of the Catechism for more information than is given in these sermons.

There is nothing unusual about preaching on the Catechism. Some of our bishops and priests did that when the Catechism first appeared in 1994–95. At the time I was living in New York City and Cardinal John J. O'Connor in St. Patrick's Cathedral preached a series of sermons based on the Catechism for a year or more.

Lay people who want to know more about their faith may find these sermons helpful. It is my hope that, having read one of them, they will be motivated to read what the Catechism has to say on the subject.

Finally, the purpose of these 54 sermons is to promote a better understanding of the beauty and depth of truth contained in our holy Catholic faith. It is my hope that this, in turn, will lead to an increase of faith, hope and charity.

—Kenneth Baker, S.J.

THE BIBLE

The Bible is a text inspired by God, entrusted to the Church for the nurturing of faith, and for guidance of the Christian life.

(Pontifical Biblical Commission, 1993)

Today I want to give you a brief introduction to the Bible. The Bible is the most important book in the world because it contains the word of God. It is a collection of letters that God has written to us to tell us where we came from, why we are here on this earth, and where we are going. It tells us what we should believe and what we must do in order to attain eternal life and eternal happiness. God is the primary author of the Bible, but he used human beings as instruments to produce it—men like Moses, David, Isaiah, Ezekiel, Matthew, Mark, Luke, John, Paul and the other prophets. In all they wrote they spoke the truth and were protected from error by the guidance of the Holy Spirit. Since God is the author the Bible also breathes forth the Holy Spirit today to enlighten our minds and inflame our hearts with love for God.

The Bible is something like a small library because it contains 73 books—46 books in the Old Testament and 27 books in the New Testament. A person who wants to read the Bible should realize that it takes effort to come to a good understanding of the contents of the Greatest Book ever written. It takes effort because the Bible was composed by many different men over a period of more than a thousand years. It was also written in ancient languages—the Old Testament in Hebrew and the New Testament in Greek. Also it was written in the Near East and reflects cultures flourishing over two thousand years ago—cultures that most of us are not familiar with. Many of its words and concepts seem strange to us, and the way of thinking is often different from Western logical and technical categories.

The Bible is the Greatest Book in the world because it has God as its author. One might look upon the 73 books as so many chapters of one book because there is one author. Since God is the author, we say that Holy Scripture is "inspired," that is, God caused it to be written, and so it has a divine origin.

The heart of the OT is what is called the "Pentateuch" or the first five books: Genesis, Exodus, Leviticus, Numbers, and Deuteronomy. There we learn that God chose Abraham to be the father of the Chosen People of Israel; he made a "covenant" or "testament" with him and promised him and his descendants his protection. That covenant is reflected on and worked out in the other books of the OT. The other major parts are the prophets like Isaiah, Jeremiah and Hosea; then there are the historical books, like the books of Kings; finally, there are the wisdom books, like Sirach, Ecclesiastes and Wisdom. They were written during a thousand years before the birth of Christ.

The New Testament you are more familiar with. The heart of the NT is the four Gospels of Matthew, Mark, Luke and John. They are the most important because they recount the life, death, resurrection and teaching of Jesus Christ, the God-Man, who came into this world to redeem us from the power of Satan and sin and so to make it possible for us to attain eternal life with God in heaven. The birth of Jesus Christ two thousand years ago is the most important event that ever took place in human history. Each of the Gospels presents Jesus in a different light so they help us to gain a fuller understanding of him. It is the same story told from different points of view.

In addition to the Gospels there is the Acts of the Apostles which gives us the history of the first forty years or so of the growth of the Catholic Church beginning in Jerusalem and going to Rome and the whole Roman Empire. The great theologian of the time was St. Paul who is the author of 14 letters in the NT. Added to that are the so-called "Catholic Epistles" of James, Peter, John and Jude. The last book is Revelation or the Apocalypse of St. John the Evangelist. That is a very brief listing of the 73 books in the OT and the NT. When taken all together they are called "the Bible," a

Greek word which means "the book." Because the author is God and it tells us about God's plan for the world, it is without doubt "the Book of books."

Reading and studying the Bible is a major enterprise. Each year hundreds of new books on the Bible are published. Every Sunday millions of Catholics hear sermons or homilies on a passage from the Bible. The Mass and the liturgy of the Church are based on it. Most universities and colleges have courses on the Bible; all the various Christian denominations promote it.

Every written text has to be interpreted and so it is with the Bible. With regard to the interpretation of the Bible, the Catholic Church insists that the fundamental meaning of the text is the literal meaning, that is, the meaning intended by the original author. That meaning is expressed in different literary forms, such as history, poetry, prayer, prophecy, wise sayings and so forth.

A second type of interpretation is what is known as the "spiritual meaning" of a text. This is a meaning that goes beyond the literal expression and points to some other reality, such as Moses and David being "types" of Jesus. In some cases, metaphor and allegory are used to arrive at a fuller meaning of a text. An example of this can be found in Matthew 1:23, where the author applies the word "virgin" from Isaiah 7:14 to the Blessed Virgin Mary. Isaiah was thinking about the wife of the king, but Matthew saw the word as a reference to Mary and the Virgin Birth of Jesus.

The unity of the Bible comes from that fact that the Holy Spirit is the author of the whole Bible. He composed it in such a way that earlier books foreshadow later events, and later event clarify former words or events that are obscure. So everything in the OT points to Jesus and the NT *in some way* since Jesus is the fulfillment of all the prophecies. On this point, St. Augustine said that the NT is hidden in the OT and the OT is made manifest in the NT.

The Bible is a sign of God's love for us. It is directed to man's mind and also to his will or heart. In addition to the instruction we find in the Bible about the Trinity, Incarnation, Church and the Sacraments, it also offers us an abundance of prayers. The 150

Psalms are called "the prayer book of the Church." Many other beautiful prayers are scattered throughout the books of the Bible besides the Psalms.

The Bible belongs to the Catholic Church. She inherited the OT from Israel and her members composed the books of the NT. The Catholic Church preserved the Bible and tells us which books belong in it. The Church urges us to read it and to pray with it. St. Jerome said in the 4th century that "ignorance of Scripture is ignorance of Christ" because it is all about him. The Bible achieves its purpose in each one of us when we can pray with it and so grow in the knowledge and love of God and our neighbor.

Let me conclude with the words of the Pontifical Biblical Commission in 1993: *The Bible is a text inspired by God, entrusted to the Church for the nurturing of faith, and for guidance of the Christian life.*

REVELATION

The Bible is a holy book because it contains divine revelation, that is, communication about himself from God to man.

Today I want to explain what the Church means by "revelation." The word itself means to uncover or unveil something that is hidden. In normal conversation when one reveals something, it means that he makes known or public something that was hidden or unknown.

When we speak about revelation in the Bible and as the basis of our Catholic faith, the word refers to the disclosure to mankind by God of himself, of who he is, and of his plan in creating the world and putting man on this earth. Since God is an absolute Spirit, transcendent and not a part of this material world, his nature and his thinking are not known to us from what we see and experience in this world of time and space (see Rom. 1:18–20).

By the light of natural reason we can know something about God from the things he has created—the sun, moon, stars, living things on earth and the order of the universe. We can reason from effect to cause. But such knowledge is incomplete, and historically was often accompanied by many errors, for example, in the worship of idols or the sun.

The Bible and the tradition of the Church teach us that God revealed himself and the secrets of his will to certain individuals like Adam, Noah, Abraham, Moses, Jeremiah. He revealed himself in words and deeds and proved the truth of his words by performing great miracles. He spoke to the prophets, like Moses and Isaiah, and he worked mighty miracles such as freeing the people of Israel from the slavery in Egypt, by parting the Red Sea, by making a covenant with Moses on Mt. Sinai, by parting the River Jordan, by choosing David as King of Israel.

God's revelation of himself in the Old Testament was partial, imperfect and provisional. At that time God spoke to the prophets and they reported what they had heard. All of that was preparatory for the fullness of revelation in Jesus Christ who is the Word of God and God himself—the fullness of revelation. So in Jesus it is God himself who is speaking to us. What he said and did is written down in the four Gospels of Matthew, Mark, Luke and John. Some of the effects or consequences of that revelation are recorded for us by St. Paul and the other writers in the New Testament.

The process was: Jesus revealed himself and the will of God to his Apostles and sent them to convert the whole world; the Apostles and their co-workers preached the Gospel of Jesus and eventually wrote it down in what we call the New Testament. They established successors in appointing bishops and priests to continue the work until the end of time and the Second Coming of Christ; the Catholic Church today is the continuation of the Church established by Jesus. She is the guardian of the revelation and the only authentic interpreter of the word of God (see Vatican II, "Revelation" [DV], 10, 12).

From what has just been said, it should be clear what revelation is, where it can be found, and who guards and interprets it. My next point is to say something about the content of revelation. What does it tell us about God, the world, and my own personal reason for existence?

Vatican II in its document on divine revelation answers these questions clearly and succinctly: "It pleased God in his goodness and wisdom, to reveal himself and to make known the mystery of his will. His will was that men should have access to the Father, through Christ, the Word made flesh, in the Holy Spirit, and thus become sharers in the divine nature" (DV 2). So revelation has to do with salvation, with doing God's will in this life, and with man's future in the next life. We have "access to the Father" and "become sharers in the divine nature" by faith in Jesus Christ, by believing in him, and by living according to his commandment of love of God and neighbor. In order to help us to save our souls, he established his Church with its seven Sacraments and its preaching of the Gospel. If we accept his word and follow his example we will know the truth and the truth will make us free (John 8:31–32).

That sentence in St. John's Gospel was frequently quoted by Pope John Paul II.

It is clear from the study of the Bible that God revealed himself to man by gradually communicating the mystery of himself, not just in words, but in both words and deeds. His deeds manifest his almighty power and his love for man; the words explain the meaning of the deeds. This is true of God's great marvels in the OT and also of the birth, life, miracles, death and resurrection of Jesus. The four Gospels give an historical account of the main points in the life of Jesus. They tell us what he said and what he did and the impact he made on those who heard him and associated with him.

If God wants to communicate with us, he has to adapt himself to our way of understanding—through our words and concepts. God spoke to the prophets in the OT. Jesus Christ, who is the Second Person of the Blessed Trinity, is the Word of God incarnate. He not only spoke the word of God; he is the Word of God and he is God's last word. God's word is not like our weak words. His word is active, powerful, life-giving—it makes things happen. When Jesus speaks things happen, such as: "Take up your bed and walk"; "Lazarus, come forth"; and with a word he immediately calmed the wind and the waves on the Sea of Galilee.

The divine word of revelation is amazing and fascinating because it contains hidden within it a treasure of truth, wisdom and knowledge. When God speaks to man, whether in the preparation stage of the OT or in the fulfillment stage of the NT, he has a RELIGIOUS purpose in mind, that is, man's destiny to be united with God forever in a union of love.

How did divine revelation get to us? Jesus is the fullness of the revelation of God. He communicated it to the Apostles and commissioned them to preach it to the whole world (Matt. 28:18–20). The Apostles and apostolic men, under the inspiration of the Holy Spirit, committed the message of salvation to writing; they appointed bishops as their successors and handed over their teaching role to them (DV 7) to be continued in the Church until the end of the world.

Our Catholic faith tells us that Scripture is "inspired" by God. So inspiration refers to the divine origin of Scripture. This means that the Holy Spirit "breathes" through Scripture to us, that is, he is the author and he guarantees the truth of the Bible. Since God is the author, it follows that Scripture is free from all errors. Therefore, Scripture teaches without error the truth which God wanted put into the sacred writings for the sake of our salvation (DV 11).

The Bible is the Church's own book or story. The Church produced it, preserved it, and only she knows what it truly means. Quotes from the Bible are used in all the Sacraments, especially in the readings and prayers contained in the Roman Missal. Preaching and catechetics must also be nourished and regulated by Holy Scripture. The Church has the highest regard for the Bible. Vatican II said: "The Church has always venerated the divine Scriptures, just as she venerates the body of the Lord" (DV 21).

Through divine revelation we know that God is love, that he is our Creator and Redeemer, that out of love for us he sent his Only-begotten Son into this world to tell us how to get to heaven and to show us the way. God is just, but he is also a God of compassion and mercy. The most important points of revelation are contained in the Nicene Creed which we pray at each Sunday Mass. As a sign of our faith in divine revelation, we should say "Amen" with conviction when we pray the Creed at today's Mass.

FAITH

"The just man lives by faith"

(Rom. 1:17)

The three most important virtues in the life of a Christian are faith, hope and charity. They are called "theological" virtues because they have God as their object. Today let us reflect on the meaning of faith.

For our eternal salvation, in order to attain the face to face vision of God, faith in Jesus Christ as Messiah and Son of God is absolutely necessary. St. Paul tells us in Romans 1:17 that "The just man lives by faith." The primary model of faith in the Old Testament is Abraham. St. Paul says of him in Romans 4:3, "Abraham believed God and it was reckoned to him as righteousness." The Gospel of Jesus Christ is "the power of God for salvation to every one who has faith, to the Jew first and also the Greek" (Rom. 1:16).

St. Paul defines faith for us in Hebrews 11:1 when he says, "Faith is the assurance of things hoped for, the conviction of things not seen." And a few verses later he adds, "Without faith it is impossible to please God. For whoever would draw near to God must believe that he exists and rewards those who seek him" (11:6).

The very first words of Jesus in the Gospel of Mark have to do with faith: "... Jesus came into Galilee, preaching the gospel of God, and saying, 'The time is fulfilled, and the kingdom of God is at hand; repent and believe in the gospel'" (1:14–15). In most cases Jesus makes faith the condition of his miracles. For example, he requires faith of his good friend Martha before he raises her brother Lazarus from the dead.

Let us examine the idea of faith more closely. St. Thomas Aquinas says that faith is the assent of the mind to truths revealed by God and that assent is moved by the will influenced by divine grace (S.Th. II-II, 2, 1). There are two main aspects of faith: what is believed (objective) and the personal act of belief (subjective). In the objective sense faith is the content of revelation contained in the Bible, Tradition and the Magisterium of the Church and is expressed in the various Creeds of the Church. In the subjective sense faith is an act of the intellect—the assent of the mind to truth revealed by God and that assent is moved by the will influenced by grace.

Faith is not something we merit; it is a free gift from God. The theological virtue of faith is infused with divine grace at Baptism, along with the other virtues. When a person falls into mortal sin, he or she loses sanctifying grace and charity, but he does not lose faith, unless he sins against faith by denying it in an act of apostasy. Here we see the danger of books and movies like *The Da Vinci Code*. It is obvious that the author, Dan Brown, has lost his faith and is trying to influence others to reject the faith of the Catholic Church.

The conscious motive for positing the act of faith is or needs to be the authority of God revealing who is seen by the intellect to be absolutely truthful and is embraced by the will as the absolute good. The miracles of Jesus and the Apostles make the faith credible because they are obviously worked by God in testimony to the truth of what Jesus and the Apostles said.

Here are the main characteristics of faith. 1) Faith is *obscure* because we do not understand fully the various propositions of faith, such as the Trinity, Incarnation and Grace. 2) Faith is absolutely *certain* because it is based on the authority of God revealing who knows all things, is infinite truth and so cannot deceive anyone. 3) Faith is *free* because the will, influenced by grace, commands the mind to assent. 4) Faith is *supernatural* because it is moved by the grace of God and its purpose is to attain a supernatural end—the face to face vision of God. 5) Faith is *necessary* in order to attain the purpose for which God created us—union with him in heaven.

The main object of faith is belief in Jesus Christ as the divine Son of God, Messiah and Savior of all mankind. Jesus reveals to us the mystery of the Holy Trinity—Father, Son and Holy Spirit. We believe that Jesus is both God and man. This is the great mystery of the Incarnation of God in Jesus Christ.

Jesus is fully human because he was born of the Virgin Mary and is a descendant of King David. He was born in Bethlehem of Judea; he preached, suffered, died and rose again on the third day.

Jesus is also God—the Second Person of the Blessed Trinity. We see this in his "I am" statements, such as: "Truly, truly, I say to you, before Abraham was, I am" (John 8:58). He identifies himself with the Father when he says, "The Father and I are one" (John 10:30), and also, "He who sees me sees the Father" (John 14:9). One of the reasons why he was put to death by the Jewish leaders was that he claimed to be God and they considered that blasphemy.

Faith in Jesus implies faith in everything he taught us himself, as recorded in the Gospels, and what he taught through his Apostles whom he endowed with the fullness of the Holy Spirit on Pentecost.

Jesus established a hierarchical Church on Peter and the Apostles: "As the Father has sent me, even so I send you" (John 20:21); and, "Thou art Peter and on this rock I will build my Church..." (Matt. 16:18). So the Church has authority from Christ to teach, to sanctify and to rule the faithful. Because the Holy Spirit dwells in her, the Church is infallible in teaching matters of faith and morals.

Jesus, through his Church, is the only source of salvation. In the Acts of the Apostles we read, "And there is salvation in no one else, for there is no other name under heaven given among men by which we must be saved" (4:12). The Church communicates the grace and salvation of Christ to us through the preaching of the word and the Seven Sacraments.

Since we are dealing with divine mysteries that totally surpass human understanding, the content of our faith is inexhaustible. This means that we can always learn more about our faith by study of the Bible, the history of the Church and the lives of the saints.

One who lives by faith, trusts in God and obeys his command-ments. To grow in faith, one must also make frequent acts of faith, such as, "Jesus I trust in you" or "Lord, increase my faith."

To grow stronger in faith, we should pray every day: "O my God, I firmly believe that thou art one God in three divine Persons—Father, Son and Holy Spirit. I believe that thy divine Son became Man and died for our sins and that He will come again to judge the living and the dead. I believe these and all the truths which the holy Catholic Church teaches, because thou hast revealed them, who canst neither deceive nor be deceived."

HOPE

"Christ is our hope"

(1 Tim. 1:1)

The second theological virtue that has God as its object is hope. The word "hope" is certainly a good word and has a very positive meaning. Hope refers to some good that one desires, and often expects to obtain in the future. The hoped-for good must be possible of attainment, but it may also be difficult to obtain.

I am not aware of any negative connotations of the word, such as we find in the related virtues of faith and love. Once I saw in a foreign port an American mercy ship which was a floating hospital. The ship was gleaming white and the name of the ship was painted in huge red letters on the side of the hull: H O P E. That ship offered hope of medical treatment and cure to poor suffering individuals in third-world countries.

Since as Christians we live on two levels of the natural and the supernatural, there are two kinds of hope: natural and supernatural. By natural hope we mean the desire and expectation of getting some future good either by our own efforts or by the help of someone else. Many people spend their hard-earned money on lottery tickets in the hope of winning millions of dollars. Joe may hope to get a new job, to find a new house or car at a low price. He relies on his own efforts to achieve his goal. That is what I mean by natural hope.

Supernatural hope is the confident desire and expectation of getting to heaven and eternal happiness with the help of God's grace. Since the end is supernatural, the means to it are also supernatural. Therefore, the means to the end must come from God who is their only source. The motive for supernatural hope is the goodness of God, his mercy, his promises and his almighty power. For if God promises something, like eternal life, I have absolute certainty that I will get it if I follow his rules and directions. We find hope of this kind in all the saints, especially the martyrs for the faith.

Supernatural hope is *certain* because it is based on the goodness and promises of God; it is *reasonable* because of the power of God to do what he says he will do. Hope is *supernatural* because the desired good, the face to face vision of God, is supernatural and it is *necessary* because heaven is man's ultimate end.

Supernatural hope is infused into the soul by God at Baptism along with sanctifying grace. As a virtue, it is a good habit which helps us to make acts of hope, such as "Jesus I trust in you" as recommended by St. Faustina. The Psalms and St. Paul urge us again and again to trust in the Lord, to hope in the Lord, to rely on the Lord.

Who has hope and who does not have hope? Since hope is necessary for eternal salvation, those of us who are pilgrims on this earth must have hope of attaining our eternal reward. But you cannot hope for what you already possess. So the saints in heaven do not have hope because they have already attained the end of eternal happiness. The souls in purgatory have hope of seeing God face to face when they have made satisfaction for their sins. The damned in hell do not have any hope because they know that their condemnation is eternal and irreversible.

There are two sins against the virtue of hope: presumption and despair. Presumption is an inordinate trust in the mercy of God and is based on pride in the sense that one thinks God is so good that he could not condemn me to hell for my sins and will surely give me a chance to repent and go to confession before I die. This is a very common attitude today, especially among the young. They make light of mortal sin and think that God is such a "good guy" that he could not send anyone to hell. Illogically, many believe in heaven but not in hell.

The opposite extreme is despair, which is an absence of trust in the mercy of God and the conviction that one's sins are so great that God could not forgive them. Despair characterizes the state of the souls in hell because they have no repentance and know that God will never forgive them.

In order to grow in the virtue of hope the serious Catholic should realize that no created thing can completely fill the heart of man, in whom God has placed an infinite capacity for the good. As *The Imitation of Christ* says in the very first chapter: "The eye is not filled by seeing nor is the ear filled with hearing." Christian hope reminds us that all the sufferings of this life are as nothing in comparison with the glory to be manifested in us (see Rom. 8:13).

The serious Catholic will strive to cultivate the virtue of hope by intensifying as much as possible confidence in God and in his divine assistance. To achieve this confidence it helps not to be too anxious about the material things of this world, to pray daily, and to receive the Sacraments often.

Those who are advanced in the virtue of hope have confidence in God in all situations and as a result lead a life of peace and serenity, even in the midst of trials and tribulations. For those who are advanced in hope heaven begins already on earth. The saints desire to die and go to heaven, but in reality their life in heaven has already begun on earth. Their citizenship is now in heaven (see Phil 3:20).

St. Paul said that "Christ Jesus is our hope" (1 Tim. 1:1) and "Our God is the God of hope" (Rom. 15:13). Because we are Catholic Christians, because we are followers of Jesus Christ, we are a people of hope. Through our faith, hope and love we know for sure that we will attain the Beatific Vision, the face to face vision of God in total happiness for all eternity if we remain faithful to him and keep his commandments.

With this in mind we should make at least one act of hope every day in these words: "O my God, relying on thy infinite goodness and promises, I hope to obtain the pardon of my sins, the help of thy grace, and life everlasting through the merits of Jesus Christ, my Lord and Redeemer. Amen."

Just as you can never have too much faith and too much love of God, so also you can never have too much hope in our God of mercy and love.

CHARITY

"God is love, and he who abides in love abides in God, and God abides in him"

(1 John 4:16)

It has been said that love makes the world go around. There is a lot of truth in that statement. Everything we do or desire is motivated by love in one way or another. St. John says in his First Letter that God is love and he who abides in love abides in God and God in him (1 John 4:16). It was because of his love that God created the world and each one of us; it was because of his love that he sent his only-begotten Son, Jesus Christ, to be our Savior and Redeemer.

The final purpose of our existence is to get to heaven and to be eternally happy in the face to face vision of God. That is a permanent state of friendship with the source of all goodness.

The family is the basic building block of society. The family and human life are about love. Ideally the family results from the love of a man and woman for each other—a fruitful love that generates children and new members of the human family.

In everything we do we seek the good—either for ourselves or for others. Wishing goodness for others is what we mean by love or charity. When we love someone we wish them well.

I want to talk to you today about charity or supernatural love for God. First, I would like to explain the meaning of natural love; then I will apply that to charity or supernatural love.

In its purest sense, love means willing what is good for another person. Love is an act of the human will whose object is always what is good. Also, we like and desire material things, but we do not love them in the full sense of the word "love." There are two kinds of love: Love of concupiscence and love of friendship. Love of concupiscence means that I love someone for what he or she can do for me: give pleasure such as a golf partner, or utility – someone who can help me get a new job or earn more money. Love of friendship means that I wish the goodness and well-being of a friend for his own sake, and not for what I can get out of it. It means sacrificing oneself for the good of another. We find this love in families where parents sacrifice their own good for the good of their children. It is also called "the love of benevolence." This love resides in the will, not in the emotions or feelings. This is the kind of love God has for us. Charity or the love of God means that we affirm the goodness of God; we praise him for his goodness. This attitude is expressed in the Our Father when we pray "Hallowed be thy name," "Thy will be done."

Charity means to love God for himself, because of his fullness of being and infinite goodness. God created the world and me because of his love; he did it to communicate his own being and goodness to others. Creation is totally altruistic, since God does not get anything out of it; he gives, he does not get.

All non-personal creatures below man—minerals, plants and animals—praise God by their very being, by doing what they were created to do. Only man has an intellect and free will with which he can know God and relate to him in a personal way. Man, since he has a free will, can freely worship God or freely reject Him. The angels can do that, but in the material universe only man enjoys the freedom to obey or not to obey God. Some angels rebelled, and they became devils; Adam rebelled and so lost his immortality and friendship with God.

Jesus Christ, who is the incarnate God on earth, calls us his friends. He died for us because he loves us and seeks a return of love. He promises to abide with us if we keep his commandment to love God and our neighbor "If a man loves me, he will keep my word, and my Father will love him, and we will come to him and make our abode with him" (John 14:23).

We should love God because we were made for love and God loves us. He is our greatest benefactor because he has given us everything we have—body and soul, life, the air we breathe, food, drink, family, friends, the Church and the Sacraments. God seeks love from us – that is his first commandment, but he does not force us; he will not violate the freedom he has given us. Jesus died for us out of love for us: The Sacred Heart is a visible symbol of his love—a heart pierced by a spear on Calvary. The 27 books of the New Testament are love letters to man.

As children we learn how to love from our parents and family. When others love us we want to love them in return. A little reflection shows us that God loves us, so we should love him in return. We show love for God by doing his will. We can prove our love for God by keeping his commandments, by daily prayer, by reception of the Sacraments, especially Eucharist and Penance, and by showing love for our neighbor. Why love of neighbor? Love of God implies love of neighbor because of his dignity—God loves him and has destined him for eternal life just as he has destined me to eternal life.

Charity as a habit of the will is infused into the soul by God at Baptism along with sanctifying grace. Grace elevates the soul to the supernatural level and makes us a "new creature," as St. Paul says. Charity is infused into the will as an operative habit and is distinct from sanctifying grace. Charity is one of the three theological virtues which have God as their object—faith, hope and charity. Grace and charity always go together—they are inseparable. So when a person commits a mortal sin, he loses both sanctifying grace and charity. The reason is that every mortal sin is a rejection of God and his dominion over us. Grace and charity are regained by contrition, confession and absolution in the Sacrament of Penance.

Divine grace received from Baptism and the other Sacraments makes us friends of God, children of God and heirs of Heaven. Charity makes us pleasing to God—we are returning his love. Some of the effects of charity are: joy, peace, patience, kindness, generosity, faithfulness, gentleness and self control (see Gal. 5:22).

Charity can always be increased—you can never have too much. We see an abundance of it in Our Blessed Mother, in the Apostles and saints. Charity is increased by good works such as: prayer, Sacraments, self-denial, almsgiving, acts of faith, hope and charity, and offering daily short prayers such as "Jesus I trust in you,"; "Lord Jesus Christ, Son of the living God, have mercy on me a sinner"; "Most Sacred Heart of Jesus I implore that I may ever love thee more and more."

Charity or the love of God, and the grace that goes with it, is our most precious possession. Charity makes us a close friend of God who is the source of all good and the giver of eternal life to those who respond to his love. He is eternal and permanent. All earthly things are temporal and passing away—they are like the dust or ashes put on our forehead on Ash Wednesday.

We all seek love and permanent life. Charity is the greatest of all the virtues because it guarantees eternal life for us and eternal life with God is the only thing that can fully satisfy our desire for happiness. Our greatest happiness in this life results from love of other persons and being loved in return. There is a special spiritual happiness, along with peace and joy, that is the fruit of loving God and being a friend of the one who is the source of all goodness and beauty.

I conclude our consideration on charity or divine love with the words of St. Paul in 1 Corinthians 13:12–13: "Now we see in a mirror, dimly, but then we shall see face to face. Now I know only in part; then I will know fully, even as I have been fully known. And now faith, hope and love abide, these three; and the greatest of these is love." Amen.

CREED: ARTICLE 1

"I believe in God, the Father almighty,
Creator of heaven and earth."

The Apostles' Creed, which we say at the beginning of the Rosary, contains twelve articles of our Catholic faith. The Creed is a summary of our faith in God and Jesus Christ. I am going to preach a series of twelve sermons on the Creed, with the intention of bringing home to you a better understanding of our holy Catholic faith. The same truths are expressed also in the Nicene Creed which we recite each Sunday after having heard the sermon, but they are given in more detail.

Each word in the first article is full of meaning: "I believe in God, the Father almighty, Creator of heaven and earth." The word "believe" does not mean "to think" or "to have an opinion" about something. It expresses the deepest conviction by which the human mind gives firm assent to truths revealed by God. To believe is to make an act of faith. St. Paul says that faith is "the conviction of things hoped for, the assurance of things not seen" (Heb. 11:1). Faith is certain and excludes all doubt, but it is also obscure because we affirm truths we do not fully understand, such as the Holy Trinity and the Real Presence of Jesus in the Eucharist. God's grace—a free gift—is necessary for the act of faith; grace assists the will to move the mind to make the act of faith and illumines the mind to help it grasp the mysteries. We considered this in detail in a former sermon on faith.

The object of our faith is God whom we do not see with our eyes; we cannot hear him speak and we cannot touch him with our hands. But we know he is real because we can see his effects in the order and beauty of the universe: in the sun, the moon, the stars, the plants, the animals, and fellow human beings. We learn about him from our parents, from the Church and from our teachers. Man can learn something about God by reason and philosophy, but that knowledge is not very clear and tends to be subject to many errors. It is much easier to get correct knowledge about God through faith; it is also clearer and more certain, because it is based on the word of God who is infinite goodness and truth and so he cannot lie or deceive.

By the word "God" we mean an infinite being who is unique—there is only one God. He identifies himself to Moses in Genesis 3:14 when he gives his name as "I am who am." God is infinite in being, so he has no beginning or end; he is the fullness of all perfections—existence, knowledge, goodness, truth, power, eternity, and every other positive virtue. We will see later on that the one God is a trinity of persons—Father, Son and Holy Spirit. The Church expresses this by saying that God is one in substance or nature but at the same time a community of three Persons. This is the most basic of all Christian mysteries. When he gave us the fundamental prayer to God, the "Our Father," Jesus taught us to call God "Father." A father is one who generates new beings; he is a source of life.

"Father" applied to God has three meanings: 1) He is called "Father" because he is the Creator and Ruler of the universe, that is, he is the source of everything that exists in the universe; 2) He is also the Father of Jesus Christ in the strict sense, since Jesus is the only-begotten Son of the Father; so Jesus shares the same nature as the Father—he is God from God and "consubstantial" with the Father as we say in the Nicene Creed; 3) He is also called "Father" because he adopts Christians as his children through the grace of Jesus Christ. Here we have a hint of the truth of the Trinity, since father is a relational term which implies a son; Jesus is that Son in the full sense; he is not an adopted son or child as we are.

The Bible often calls God "almighty," that is, infinite in power or power without limit. In Gen. 17:1 we read, "I am the almighty Lord." In Luke 1:37 we read, "For with God nothing will be impossible," that is, he can do all things—there are no limits to his power. He created all things by an act of his will and sustains them in existence. We see a reflection of this power in Jesus who cures many people with a word and raises them from the dead. Our Blessed Mother also gives expression to this truth when she says in her *Magnificat*, "he who is mighty has done great things for me" (Luke 1:49). So this attribute applies to each of the Three Persons; we confess that the Father is almighty, the Son is almighty and the Holy Spirit is almighty, and yet there are not three almighties but only one almighty. That is because they are equal in being, majesty and power.

God is the creator and source of everything that exists—the whole universe and everything in it. This power is included in the fact that God is "almighty." To create means to produce things with no pre-existing material; it is usually expressed by saying that God creates "out of nothing" and nothing here does not mean "some thing." It means "no thing." When he creates, God gives limited existence to things other than himself; he himself is unlimited existence, infinite existence. He is so magnificent that we can grasp him only in negative terms by saying that he is "not finite"; we are finite and he is not what we are.

As Creator, God can do everything that is possible. In himself he has an idea of everything that is made, since each limited thing is a reflection of some aspect of the divine infinite being. Consequently, God knows everything he has made and he directs the universe by his divine Providence. We are all in the palm of his hand. But we must remember that God is infinite goodness. St. John says that God is love—that is his nature (1 John 4:16). Since he is love, he created us out of his love and he did it freely; there is no necessity in God to create the world. The world is not eternal—it had a beginning: "In the beginning God created the heavens and the earth" (Gen. 1:1). When we think of God as our Creator, the thought should fill us with wonder and amazement. It is amazing that anything should exist—it is a matter of wonder that I exist.

When the Creed says that God created "heaven and earth" this means everything that exists, both visible and invisible, as it is expressed in the Nicene Creed at Mass. The word "heaven" includes not only the sun, moon and stars, but also the holy angels who exist in nine choirs and probably number in the millions.

Here is the way the Psalmist expresses this truth: "The heavens are thine, the earth also is thine; the world and all that is in it, thou has founded them" (Ps. 89:11). God did not just create everything and then let it go its own way. He directs all things and keeps or conserves them in existence. If God did not support each thing constantly, it would vanish into nothingness.

I must add in conclusion that creation is the common work of the Three Divine Persons, since all the works of God outside of the inner divine life are common to all three Persons. Scripture says that the Father is the Creator of heaven and earth; it also says of the Son that "all thing were made by him" (John 1:3) because he is the Wisdom of God; and of the Holy Spirit it is said that "the spirit of God moved over the waters" (Gen. 1:2).

I hope this brief explanation helps you to understand better what is meant when you pray: "I believe in God, the Father almighty, Creator of heaven and earth."

CREED: ARTICLE 2

"and in Jesus Christ, his only Son, our Lord"

In the second article of the Creed we express our faith in Jesus Christ as the only Son of God, our LORD. Since he is Lord, he is God and Creator of all things in the same sense as his Father is God. Today we will reflect on four titles: Jesus, Christ, only Son, and Lord.

The name "Jesus" means "God saves" or simply, "Savior." This name was given to him by the Father in heaven when he sent his angel to Mary and Joseph. Both of them were told to give the child the name of "Jesus." As often in the Bible, the name indicates his function or role in God's plan of salvation.

Why is he called Savior? Whom is he saving? And from what is he saving? He saves us, all human beings, from sin and the consequences of sin. Because of the sin of Adam we come into this world without the grace of God and we are subject to ignorance, suffering and death. In addition, we add to that our own personal sins. Jesus saves us from that by his passion, death and resurrection embraced out of his love for us; through Jesus we are reconciled to the Father, we receive grace through faith and Baptism, and so share in the life of Christ and, as his brothers and sisters and members of his Mystical Body, we are children of God and heirs of heaven.

The name of Jesus had supreme importance among the first Christians. We see this especially in the Acts of the Apostles. There Peter cured a lame man "in the name of Jesus Christ the Nazarene" (Acts 3:6). When questioned about this by Jewish officials Peter said: "And there is salvation in no one else, for there is no other name under heaven given among men by which we must be saved" (4:12). So God has given Jesus "the name which is above all other names" (Phil. 2:9). Thus, we can call Jesus of Nazareth both Lord and God, as St. Thomas did in the Upper Room (John 20:28).

The name of our Savior is "Jesus Christ." The word "Christ" means "the anointed one." It is a Greek word which translates the Hebrew "Messiah" or anointed one. The point here is that the kings of Israel and the High Priests were anointed with oil as a sign of their consecration to God. In the Old Testament there are many prophecies that God would send a Messiah or Anointed One who would save Israel from her enemies. Jesus is that Messiah and therefore he is called "Christ."

Jesus himself, during his earthly life, was very reserved in his attitude to this title because at the time it was understood as a political or military leader. He had to teach his disciples, especially in the Gospel of Mark, that he is a "suffering Messiah" and not a political king. After the Resurrection, the first believers used the title "Christ" to sum up all the other titles. Gradually, what was once just a title became practically a proper name. Thus St. Paul constantly refers to him as "Jesus Christ" or "Christ Jesus" (cf. 1 Cor. 1:1–9). The title-name was so important that within a few years the followers of Jesus were designated by it. St. Luke tells us in Acts 11:26, "It was at Antioch that the disciples were first called Christians."

The Creed says that Jesus is "the only Son" of God the Father. Much divine truth is hidden in this brief phrase. The first is that God has a Son; since a son is of the same nature as his father, this means that Jesus is God—he is equal to the Father. The word "only" here means that Jesus is unique; he is the perfect image of the Father. The Holy Spirit is also a divine Person who proceeds from the Father and the Son, but he does not proceed in the same way that Jesus does; he proceeds from the love between the Father and the Son.

God has only one Son and that is Jesus. The Nicene Creed adds that he is "the only-begotten" Son of the Father and develops the idea more than the Apostles' Creed: it says that Jesus is "the Only Begotten Son of God, born of the Father before all ages, God from God, Light from Light, true God from true God, begotten, not made, consubstantial with the Father; through him all things were made." Just as "to be a father" means to have generated someone, so also "to be a son" means that one has been generated by someone. In our Catholic faith we believe that the relationship between Jesus and God the Father is a relationship of Son to Father. Here we have two distinct Persons, but only one God. Both the Father and the Son share in the same divine nature. The Son resembles the Father in everything; he has everything the Father has except to be Father. This is a profound truth and requires patience in study, reflection and prayer in order to fully understand the teaching of the Church on this great mystery of our holy faith.

The fourth title given to Jesus in this second article of the Creed is that he is "our Lord." When Jesus is called "Lord" it is the same thing as saying that he is God. In the Greek Old Testament the Hebrew name of God was translated as "Kyrios" which means "Lord" in English. The New Testament uses this title of "Lord" for both the Father and for Jesus, which is a way of recognizing that Jesus is God almighty. In his famous television series, Archbishop Fulton J. Sheen often referred to Jesus as "Our Blessed Lord."

When St. Thomas realizes who Jesus is after the resurrection, he falls down in worship and says to him, "My Lord and my God" (John 20:28). It cannot be any clearer than that. By attributing to Jesus the divine title "Lord," the creeds of the Church affirm from the beginning that the power, honor, and glory due to God the Father are due also to Jesus, because "he was in the form of God."

Since Jesus is God, he is worthy of adoration. He is our Savior and our Lord. "The Church... believes that the key, the center, and the purpose of the whole of man's history is to be found in its Lord and Master" because he is the God-Man who came into this world to save us from our sins and to make it possible for us to attain eternal life and happiness by faith in him. (see CCC 446–450). So we should rejoice in the thought and realization that we are Christians, and followers of "Jesus Christ, His only Son, our Lord."

CREED: ARTICLE 3

"Who Was Conceived by the Holy Spirit, and Born of the Virgin Mary"

In the first two articles of the Creed we express our faith in God the Father as our Creator, and in Jesus Christ as his only-begotten Son and our Lord. Today we will reflect on the earthly and human origins of Jesus Christ, our Savior. We ask: How did the Son of God become a man? Is he a member of the human race? Is he truly human as we are? The third article of the Creed answers these questions by saying that he was conceived by the power of the Holy Spirit and was born of the Virgin Mary.

Now we will reflect on a miraculous conception, on the Holy Spirit who is the Third Person of the Blessed Trinity, and on Mary of Nazareth who lived two thousand years ago in Galilee in the Middle East. The Creed also says that Jesus was born of a virgin mother. How can a woman be both virgin and mother? From this you can see that this article of the Creed contains and affirms many divine mysteries.

Jesus, the Son of God, was conceived or took flesh in the womb of the Virgin Mary. By these words the Church rejects the errors of those who taught that Jesus only *appeared* to be a man, but did not actually assume a real human nature (they are called docetists). Jesus was conceived without the agency of a human father or male sperm, for the Creed says that he was conceived of the *virgin* Mary. This statement rejects the error of those who said Jesus had a celestial body, but not a human, material body. One heretic (Valentinus) said that Jesus' body passed through the Virgin without receiving anything from her, just as water passes through a canal. The meaning of the Creed is that Mary supplied to Jesus everything that an ordinary mother supplies to her child in the area of nutrition and gestation. The normal nine months of the development of the Child are recognized by the liturgy of the Church, since we celebrate his conception on March 25, the Annunciation when it happened, and on Christmas, December 25, nine months later, when he was born in a cave in Bethlehem.

Jesus was conceived by the power of the Holy Spirit. There were no marital relations involved in the conception of Jesus (see Luke 1:34). It was accomplished by the power of God properly disposing matter within the womb of the Virgin Mary so that an ovum supplied by her was fertilized. This is a miracle and a great mystery. The Holy Spirit, however, is not the "father" of Jesus. In his human nature, Jesus did not have a father. To be a father means to generate in one's own likeness. The Holy Spirit, being God, does not generate Jesus' human nature in his own likeness, for the Holy Spirit is infinitely above human nature. All activity of God outside the Trinity is common to all three Persons, but some actions are attributed to one Person rather than to another. The Holy Spirit is the love of the Father and the Son, and since the Incarnation flows from the love of God for man, the formation of Christ's flesh is fittingly ascribed to the Holy Spirit.

Of those things that are common to all three Persons, Sacred Scripture often attributes some to one person, some to another. Thus, to the Father they attribute power over all things; to the Son, wisdom; to the Holy Spirit, love. Therefore, since the Incarnation manifests the boundless love of God for us, it is attributed to the Holy Spirit. It must be emphasized that God did not force Mary to be mother of the Savior. She was asked politely by the angel Gabriel and, assisted by the fullness of grace, freely assented to be the Mother of God when she said, "Behold the handmaid of the Lord. Let it be done unto me according to thy word." In that instant, God supplied by his divine power the male contribution to the conception of a child and Mary became pregnant with Jesus.

Jesus was "born of the Virgin Mary." Next the Creed tells us that Mary of Nazareth is the mother of Jesus—and that she was a virgin. This is unheard of and a great miracle that a woman could give birth without pain and without breaking her virginal integrity. Here we see the humility and love of God that he should humble himself to become a helpless child, totally dependent on his mother. So God came into this world the same way each one of us did. And why? Because of his infinite love for us and to save us from our sins. This statement also locates the birth of Jesus in a certain family, at a certain place and time—two thousand years ago in Galilee. Mary and her husband, Joseph, belonged to the tribe of Juda, and were descended from King David, and it was predicted in the OT that the Messiah would be a descendant of King David. Jesus was born in Bethlehem, the city of David.

Mary was chosen by God to be the mother of the Savior. At the Annunciation, the angel Gabriel addresses her as "full of grace"; the Church concludes from that and from other texts in the Bible that Mary herself was conceived free of original sin. This is called her "Immaculate Conception." By the grace of God Mary was kept free from all sin, so the power of Satan could not touch or come close to Jesus who is the Son of God and God in the flesh. She is the Immaculate Virgin Mary.

The Church believes that Mary was "always" a virgin, that is, she was a virgin before, during and after the birth of Jesus. So when the gospels say that certain individuals were the "brothers and sisters" of Jesus, this means that they were cousins or relatives. Mary had only one child and that was Jesus by a miraculous conception and a miraculous birth; for that reason we call her "the Blessed Virgin Mary."

There are many salutary lessons to be drawn from the conception and birth of Jesus. He is born of a virgin; he is born in poverty; he is born a stranger under a roof not his own; he is placed in a crib in the presence of animals. He has assumed our human nature and become one of us to lead us to heaven. He did not do that for the angels, but he did it for us. At Christmas we commemorate all these truths.

God became man and was born in Bethlehem in order to give us a spiritual rebirth through his grace and sacraments. There was no room for him at the inn in Bethlehem. We should make room for him now by welcoming him into our hearts and souls so he can communicate his divine life to us—so that he can make us adopted children of God and heirs of heaven.

CREED: ARTICLE 4

"Suffered under Pontius Pilate, was Crucified, Died and Was Buried"

These few words summarize the last day of the Life of Jesus. These events are commemorated in a special, solemn way in the ancient ceremonies of Holy Week. The fourth article of the Apostles' Creed expresses our faith in the passion and death of Jesus. As before, much truth is implied and concentrated in a few words. I will just mention in passing that the Creed does not say anything about the private and public life of Jesus—nothing about his preaching of the Good News of salvation, nothing about his miracles. All of that is passed over as we move immediately to the last day of his life in the holy city of Jerusalem.

Jesus Christ is a historical person who lived in Palestine about 2000 years ago in a part of the Roman Empire. By mentioning the Roman governor, Pontius Pilate, the Creed clearly locates the passion and death of Jesus in time and space. Pilate was governor in Judea about 30 A.D. That is a fact that can be established by profane history. Jesus, therefore, being a member of the Jewish race, was put to death under this Roman official in Palestine. Crucifixion was the most severe form of capital punishment in Roman law. It was so degrading that it could not be applied in the case of a Roman citizen; that is why St. Paul, a Roman citizen, was beheaded instead of crucified. It was reserved for slaves, robbers and brigands. Jesus had foretold what kind of death he would die when he said: "And I, if I be lifted up, will draw all things to myself" (John 12:32).

To suffer means to endure some kind of evil or harm—to endure the loss of some good. Since man is spirit in a material body, he can suffer both in his soul and in his body. In the Garden of Gethsemane, Jesus' suffering was primarily in the soul. When he suffered ridicule, scourging, the crowning of thorns, he endured harm in both body and soul. "Suffering" is a bad word for most of us. We would rather not hear the word or think about its meaning. And we shun the reality in any way we can. Just think of the billions of white, red, green and blue pills that are sold each year in this country. Most of them were invented to help people avoid some suffering.

The Creed says simply of Jesus that "he suffered." The major difference between the suffering of Jesus and our suffering is that he freely willed it and accepted it out of love for us. We are subject to suffering of all kinds because we cannot control the world around us. Jesus' situation was different. With his divine knowledge he knew everything. With his divine power he was capable of warding off any threat, and because of that power he died when he chose to. Remember what he said in Gethsemane: "Do you think that I cannot appeal to my Father, and he will at once send me more than twelve legions of angels?" (Matt. 26:53).

Why did Jesus suffer? He did it for our sake—for each one of us. Because of the first sin of Adam we were cut off from the life of grace, excluded from heaven and condemned to die. Jesus took it upon himself freely to make satisfaction for us and so to pour out the grace of God and divine life upon us.

Jesus died from his wounds and loss of blood at 3 p.m. on Good Friday. All men are under the certain, sad sentence of death, and Jesus submitted himself to that law. Death, as we know from Romans 5 and 6, is the result of sin; as St. Paul says, "The wages of sin is death" (6:23). Philosophically, death means the separation of the soul from the body. The body corrupts, but the soul lives on because it is spiritual and therefore immortal. There is both a personal and an impersonal dimension to the meaning of death. On the impersonal level, it means that biological and physical forces overpower man to such an extent that his soul can no longer animate the body. The signs of death are the cessation of biological functions, such as breathing, and the beginning of corruption. We do not know exactly when the soul leaves the body, probably in about three hours.

On the personal level, death means that our spiritual growth and our exercise of human freedom in time come to a brutal halt. As adults, we determine ourselves according to our likes and dislikes, our aspirations and our fears. In death, we are determined by powers beyond our control and contrary to our will. Man lives his whole life under the shadow of death. It is our constant companion, whether we explicitly think about it or not. Man fears death and senses, somehow, that it should not be, that it is beneath his dignity to have to submit to physical dissolution. So most people do all they can to delay the time of death.

The point here is that Jesus, the sinless One, submitted to the power of death which had no claim on him. He died our death in order to save us from eternal death of the soul and to open us up to the life of God. Thus, St. Peter says in his first letter: "Christ also died once for our sins, the just for the unjust, that he might offer us to God, being put to death indeed in the flesh, but enlivened in the spirit" (1 Pet. 3:18).

In order to convince all men that he truly died, Jesus was buried in a tomb for three days before his resurrection. He was buried according to Jewish custom in a tomb very near to Calvary. I was privileged to celebrate Mass there. In this he shared our lot, with the exception that his body was not to see corruption. This was predicted in Psalm 16:10, "You will not give your holy one to see corruption." His body could not corrupt because it was still united to the Second Person of the Blessed Trinity and therefore still worthy of adoration. After about 38 hours, his soul would be reunited to his body and he would rise gloriously from the dead as he had predicted on several occasions.

I have just given you a brief account of the Passion of Christ. It was a sacrifice most acceptable to God the Father and offered on the altar of the Cross; it is re-presented in an unbloody manner in each Mass. As St. Paul said: "Christ loved us and gave himself up for us, a fragrant offering and sacrifice to God" (Eph. 5:2). By his Passion Jesus delivered us from sin.

In the next place he rescued us from the tyranny of the devil, as Jesus says: "Now is the judgment of the world; now shall the prince of this world be cast out" (John 12:31). Jesus destroyed the eternal punishment due to our sins and reconciled us to the Father.

Finally, by taking away our sins, he opened to us heaven which had been closed by the sin of Adam. So Christ is the new Adam, assisted by Mary the new Eve, who merited for us to become new creatures through the love and grace of God.

These are some of the truths to think about when you pray the Apostles Creed: "He suffered under Pontius Pilate, was crucified, died and was buried."

CREED: ARTICLE 5

"He Descended into Hell, and on the Third Day He rose again"

After the Creed says that Jesus suffered, died and was buried, it goes on to say that "he descended into hell." The Latin says that he "descendit ad inferos," that is, he descended into the under-world—that dark, shadowy place that is mysterious to us. The hell mentioned here is not the hell of the devils. The Hebrews called it "Sheol" and the Greeks called it "Hades." After his body was in the tomb for three days—about 38 hours from Friday evening to Sunday morning—his soul was rejoined to his body and he rose gloriously from the dead. The delay of three days is to assure us that he was truly dead.

Death means the separation of the soul from the body. So the Church is telling us that, as his body lay in the tomb, his soul descended into the underworld where the souls were of all human beings, from Adam and Eve to the Good Thief. Jesus went into the underworld to preach the Gospel to the dead. Because of his infinite merits, heaven was now opened so that all those who died in the grace of God might enter heaven and enjoy the face to face vision of God.

The underworld consists of three stages or layers: the Limbo of the Fathers which would be a place of natural happiness for those who were purified and ready for heaven; purgatory where those being cleansed of personal sins were still suffering; and Hell in the sense of the place of damnation for the devils and all those who were lost. It did not include what we mean by heaven. So Jesus announced to all the dead that heaven was now open for those who died as friends of God. This phrase means that the saints of the time before Christ were now admitted to heaven, that is, all those saints like Abraham, Moses and the prophets; those in purgatory would go to heaven when they were totally purified; there is no change in the status of those in Hell; so Jesus did not free them and admit them to heaven—their damnation is permanent.

There are some beautiful paintings and works of art depicting Jesus in the underworld and leading all the saved into heaven. It is important here to remember that the Second Person of the Blessed Trinity, the Word of God, was still hypostatically united to both the soul and the body. So both body and soul were worthy of adoration during the time of their separation in death. Whole books have been written about the mysteries connected with the descent of Jesus into the underworld. We commemorate this divine event on Holy Saturday in Holy Week.

"On the third day he rose again." With these words the Creed moves from the earthly life of Our Lord to the glorious state in which he now lives. Since Jesus was buried on Friday afternoon and rose from the dead on Easter morning, his body was in the ground during some part of three days. Hence, the Creed says that he rose "on the third day," that is, the third day after his death and burial. Since this was predicted in the OT, the Nicene Creed adds here "according to the Scriptures."

The resurrection of Jesus is not like that of his friend Lazarus and the others who returned to normal human living and eventually died. No. Jesus' body and soul are now glorified with powers that we do not understand. His body is no longer limited by time and space; he can appear when and where he wishes, and then instantly disappear, as he did to the disciples in the Upper Room and as he did to the two disciples in Emmaus. The word "again" seems strange here. Normally when we use the word "again" we mean "a second or third time." It cannot mean that in the Creed, since Jesus died once and rose from the dead only once. But the word can also mean "in addition" or "on the other hand" or "however." That is what it means here. After saying that he died and was buried, the Creed says, "however," on the third day he rose from the dead.

"Resurrection" means the return of a dead man to life. So the Creed says that Jesus, who died on the Cross on Friday and whose corpse was laid in the tomb, came back to life on Sunday.

And note that he did it by his own power as he had predicted many times. This is unheard of; it is a shocking statement when you think about it. It signifies something we have never experienced, nor has anyone else; we believe it on the testimony of the Apostles, for they were the chief witnesses of the Resurrection (see Acts 2:32; 3:15; 5:32).

The Creed does not say anything about the many appearances of Jesus to his disciples during the forty days before his Ascension into heaven, but the Gospels offer many details about these appearances. In order to confirm the faith of his disciples in his Resurrection, Jesus had to convince them that it was really he. First of all, they recognized him in his physical appearance—his body was the same body, though transformed, that they had known during the preceding three years. Thomas doubted, so the Lord said to him: "Put your finger here and see my hands; and put out your hand and place it in my side; do not be faithless, but believing" (John 2:27).

Jesus also proved that he was the same Person by his mannerisms—the way he spoke, his tone of voice, the way he ate and drank and broke bread. It was really he, but in a new and transformed way of life. Jesus showed his disciples some aspects of his glory, but not all of it. For if he had shown them the fullness of his glory, it would have been too much for them. Thus, by his many appearances and gentle ways, Jesus aroused and confirmed the faith of his Apostles in his Resurrection from the dead. They saw, they touched, they knew it was the same Lord now living a new, *glorified life*. That was the purpose of the forty days before his Ascension.

Because of Jesus' Resurrection and Glorification, this passing world of suffering and death is not the same as it was before. For, one of us—a member of our human race and a descendant of Adam—has entered into the glory of God. The God-Man Jesus Christ has taken on a new spiritual existence. St. Paul says he has become "a life-giving spirit" (1 Cor. 15:45). He is "the first fruits of those who have fallen asleep" (1 Cor. 15:20). "He is the beginning, the first-born from the dead, that in everything he might be pre-eminent" (Col. 1:18).

Sin is the cause of death and all of the human suffering that surrounds it (see Rom. 5:12–21). The point of Jesus' death and Resurrection is that he has basically triumphed over sin and death. By his own death on the Cross he overcame sin, and by his glorious Resurrection from the dead he destroyed death in principle and restored man to the life that he lost in Adam. That is what the mystery of Christ is all about.

These thoughts about the descent of Jesus into the underworld, his opening of the gates of heaven and, his glorious Resurrection should help us to make fervent acts of faith, hope and charity in our divine Savior who has, by his love and grace, transformed us into adopted children of God and heirs of heaven. Most Sacred Heart of Jesus I implore that I may ever love thee more and more.

CREED: ARTICLE 6

"He Ascended into Heaven and Is Seated
at the Right Hand of the Father"

Jesus ascended into heaven from the top of the Mount of Olives in Jerusalem. On that spot there is a small, hexagonal "Church of the Ascension" which commemorates Jesus' final departure from his disciples and from this world of time and space (see Acts 1:12). In the Creed we profess our belief in Jesus' Ascension when we say, "He ascended into heaven and is seated at the right hand of the Father." Here is the way St. Mark puts it: "So then the Lord Jesus, after he had spoken to them, was taken up into heaven, and sat down at the right hand of God" (Mark 16:19).

The Ascension of Jesus into heaven is a mystery of faith, just like his Resurrection, with which it is closely associated. The event is mentioned briefly by the Evangelists Mark and Luke (24:50–53). A more detailed account is given by Luke in the Acts of the Apostles (1:1–12).

The Ascension of Jesus can be defined as the transfer of his risen, glorious body and soul to heaven, that is, to the world of the divine and the eternal. In the Old Testament God is described in some texts as "descending" from heaven to accomplish something on earth; he then "ascends" or returns to the world of the divine. Jesus himself speaks of descending to this earth and ascending again to the Father once his work of redemption has been accomplished (see John 3:13; Eph. 4:10). He also said, "And I, when I am lifted up from the earth, will draw all men to myself" (John 12:32). So the lifting up of Jesus on the cross signifies and announces his lifting up by his Ascension into heaven, and indeed begins it.

Except for the mention of the forty days by Luke in Acts, Mark, Luke and John speak of the Ascension as occurring on the day of the Resurrection. The idea is that the final glorification and exaltation of Jesus takes place at his Resurrection—they are two aspects of the same thing. Through his Resurrection-Ascension, he leaves the earth and the visible universe to take his place at the right hand of the Father in heaven.

Henceforth Christ is "seated at the right hand of the Father." This image is influenced by the Psalm 110:1, "The Lord said to my lord: 'Sit at my right hand, till I make your enemies your footstool.'" The image itself comes from the ancient world of kings and courts where the all-powerful king was surrounded by his ministers, with the most powerful and favored one sitting just to the right of the king. So by "the right hand of the Father" we understand the glory and honor of divinity, where he who sits as Son of God before all ages, indeed as God, of one being with the Father, is seated bodily after he became incarnate and his flesh was glorified.

If Jesus had not entered immediately into his final glory at the Resurrection, it would be difficult to explain where he was during the interim between the Resurrection and the Ascension. We are dealing here with a divine mystery and it is hard for us to grasp the full meaning.

There are enough indications in the Gospel accounts of the appearances of Jesus to support the belief that he was already in the glory of the Father when he appeared to his followers. But there was a period of instruction after the Resurrection during which Jesus gave his Apostles their final preparation regarding the Church and the Sacraments before going out to bear witness to him to the ends of the earth. So it is commonly believed that the Ascension means the final appearance of Jesus in his glorified humanity before his definitive departure for heaven. Thus the mystery of the Ascension has a pedagogical character.

The number "forty" in Scripture means a full period of time, a rounded-out period; it does not necessarily mean literally forty calendar days. In this context, then, it means that Jesus appeared to his disciples off and on for a period and then left them permanently. After his Ascension they had to live by faith, not by sight, and communicate with him through prayer and the sacraments.

Thus, this mystery has two aspects: 1) the heavenly glorification of the humanity of Christ which coincided with his Resurrection, and 2) his final departure from his Apostles after a period of apparitions. The feast of the Ascension, forty days after Easter, commemorates this second aspect.

The Ascension means that Jesus, triumphant over death, has begun a new life with God. He has gone to heaven to prepare a place for the elect. On the Last Day, when he comes again in glory, he will return to lead them there so that they might take up their abode with him (John14:2 ff). For this reason, the Ascension is a source of great hope and consolation for Christians.

Being seated at the Father's right hand also signifies the inauguration of the Messiah's kingdom, the fulfillment of the prophet Daniel's vision concerning the Son of man: "To him was given dominion and glory and kingdom, that all peoples, nations, and languages should serve him; his dominion is an everlasting dominion, which shall not pass away, and his kingdom one that shall not be destroyed. After this the Apostles became witnesses of the "kingdom that will have no end." They preached the Gospel to all nations and gave witness to the truth by their words, their lives, and the blood they shed for Christ.

We now live in the period of grace, the period of the Church, the period between Jesus' Ascension and his Second Coming at the end of the world. Let us thank God today for the grace we have received through the Sacraments of the Church—grace merited for us by our Lord's passion and death on the cross on Calvary. Amen.

CREED: ARTICLE 7

"From Thence He Will Come Again to
Judge the Living and the Dead"

After professing faith in the Resurrection and Ascension of Jesus at the right hand of the Father, the Creed next affirms: "And from thence he will come again to judge the living and the dead." This is also referred to as the "Second Coming" of Jesus.

Though not stressed much today, the idea of the Second Coming of Jesus occurs frequently in the New Testament. It is also called the "Day of the Lord" and the "Parousia," which means the "presence" or "arrival" of someone.

By the expression "the Second Coming," we are referring to the Christian belief in the words of Jesus that he will come again in glory at the end of the world to judge all men. The Parousia will signal the end of human history as we know it. When this will take place no one knows but the Father (Acts 1:11), nor is there any clear indication in Scripture of just how it will be accomplished. Perhaps the marvelous qualities of the resurrected body of Jesus on Easter Sunday can give us some hint of what the new world will be like.

In popular language we usually refer to these events as "the end of the world," which is itself not completely accurate, since the Day of the Lord does not mean that the universe as we know it will be <u>annihilated</u>, but only that it will be changed into something new and wonderful—something that surpasses the imagination of man.

The New Testament gives some intimations of the signs that will precede the Lord's coming to judge the world. There is mention of wars, famines, earthquakes, upheavals in the planets and stars. These "signs" are borrowed from the apocalyptic language of the Old Testament, especially as it is found in Daniel 7 and in the prophet Joel.

The Second or final Coming of Jesus in glory is contrasted with his first coming in humility as the Son of Mary and Joseph. So the Incarnation is spoken of as his first appearance to mankind. Through his Death-Resurrection-Ascension, Jesus passed from this life to a new and glorious life in heaven. From there he sends out the Holy Spirit on his Church. Now he is present in our midst through faith, through the preaching of the Gospel, in the sacraments and in the Church.

In many places, the New Testament mentions the Parousia of the Lord. For example: "They will see the Son of Man coming on the clouds of heaven" (Matt. 24:30); "If it is my will that he (John) remain until I come, what is that to you?" (John 21:23); "This Jesus... will come in the same way as you saw him go into heaven" (Acts 1:11).

To the early Christians the Second Coming of Jesus, which was understood as the consummation of God's work in redeeming the human race, was not something to be feared. Rather, it was hoped for, longed for. They fervently prayed, "Come, Lord" (I Cor. 16:22). In fact, the next-to-last sentence of the entire Bible reflects this longing, first by quoting Jesus himself, and then by adding a prayer: "'Surely I am coming soon." Amen. Come, Lord Jesus!" (Rev. 22:20). As believing, hoping followers of Jesus Christ, this should also be our prayer.

If we ask ourselves what Jesus is going to do when he comes again, we can look to the New Testament and to the Creed for the answer: He is coming to judge the living and the dead.

The thought of judgment is not very congenial to us. The notion is most usually associated with criminal courts and wrongdoing of one sort or another. There is a problem involved in deciding who is right and who is wrong, or who is guilty and who is innocent. Because we are social beings and live together in community, there are bound to be conflicts of rights. In order to resolve such conflicts there is need for judgment and judges. Though necessary, the process is painful and we would like to avoid it if at all possible.

When it comes to our relationship with God we are especially apprehensive about the prospect of being judged by him. For "all things are naked and open to his eyes," as we read in Hebrews (4:13), and not one of us is sinless.

From our catechetical instruction we know that the Church teaches a twofold judgment of God: the particular judgment that each one experiences immediately after death, and the general judgment that will take place at the end of the world or the Second Coming of Christ when the historical process will be brought to a close.

The judgment of God in this sense is the final act whereby he settles forever the destiny of the free creature—either to eternal punishment in hell or to eternal reward in heaven. The basis of God's judgment is faith and good works or charity. Those who believe and live their faith accordingly will be saved; those who believe but do not love God and neighbor will be condemned; those who refuse to believe that Jesus is the Christ and those who, not having heard about Christ, refuse the grace of God that is given to them (1 Tim. 2:4), will also be lost.

When the Creed says that Jesus will judge "the living and the dead," it means that he will judge *all* men—past, present and future. No person will escape his judgment. Since all men are subject to sin (Rom. 5), they are all likewise subject to death (Rom. 6:23). Even Jesus died, not because he was a sinner, but to carry out God's plan of redemption. Some have interpreted "the living" in the Creed to mean those in the state of grace, and "the dead" to mean those in sin. However, "the living" can also mean those who are still on this earth at the time of the Second coming. Since all men are subject to death, the most probable meaning is that they also will die and be brought before the judgment seat of Christ in an instant.

The judgment of Christ will bring to light who has believed and lived the Gospel and who has not. The Gospels make it clear that the believer has already been judged favorably and so has nothing whatever to fear from the particular or general judgment. The particular judgment will give confirmation to the individual that he or she is saved, while the general judgment will be a public manifestation of the power and the glory of Christ.

In the Creed, the explicit reference is only to the general or Last Judgment. The Church also teaches, in the Council of Florence (1439), that the particular judgment of the individual follows soon after death.

The final scrutiny will center on our faith and our love—both of God and neighbor. Jesus is our model. He also has left us a graphic description of the Last Judgment in Matthew 25:31–46. Take up your New Testament and read it. It is excellent material for reflection and meditation.

The best preparation we can make to meet our eternal Judge with confidence is to be a faithful, practicing Catholic. In concrete terms that means that we attend Mass when it is required, receive the Sacraments regularly, pray every day, and try to practice the love of God and neighbor in accordance with the grace that God gives us. Catholics who do that can face death and judgment with confidence in the mercy of God and hope for the eternal happiness Our Lord has promised to those who follow him. They can pray with the early Christians, "Marana tha," that is, "Come, Lord Jesus."

CREED: ARTICLE 8

"I Believe in the Holy Spirit"

Of the three divine Persons in the Trinity, the most mysterious one and the most difficult one for us to understand is the Holy Spirit. We can think about God the Father as the source of all things. We can even imagine him as a kindly and merciful Father. In the case of Jesus, the Son of God, we are dealing with a man like us who lived two thousand years ago in Palestine. In the Gospels we find an account of his life and teaching so we can not only think about him, but we can also use our imagination to picture him and to follow him through his earthly life. This is especially true for those who have had the good fortune to visit the Holy Land.

When it comes to the Holy Spirit, however, the matter becomes more difficult. Since the Holy Spirit has not assumed any bodily form, it is impossible for us to imagine him in any concrete way. True, certain symbols are associated with him in Scripture, but they remain mysterious. At his baptism in the Jordan the Spirit of God descended on Jesus in the form of a dove (Matt. 3:16). The Spirit is also associated with water, wind, fire, anointing, seal, hand and the finger of God. In Christian art we often see the Holy Spirit represented under these forms. But still it is hard for us to think of the Holy Spirit as a third divine Person distinct from the Father and the Son.

Nevertheless, we know from Scripture, especially from the New Testament, that in addition to the Father and the Son, there is a third divine Person in the unity of the Godhead who is fully divine and equal to the Father and the Son. Scripture calls him the "Spirit," "the Spirit of God," "the Spirit of Jesus," "the Holy Spirit," the "gift" of God, the "advocate." These are some of the titles applied to the third Person of the blessed Trinity. This truth has been enshrined in the various creeds of the Church and in numerous official documents of the councils of the Church.

So we begin the third part of the Creed by affirming: "I believe in the Holy Spirit." The Spirit is called "holy" because he proceeds from the Father, is consubstantial with the Father as the third Person in the Trinity, and is the source of sanctification of the faithful. The Holy Spirit is also said to be "the Lord." We have already seen that Jesus Christ is called the "one Lord" in the second part of the Creed. Why then use the same title with regard to the Holy Spirit? As was explained in that article, the title "Lord" is an affirmation of divinity, since its application derives from the use of "Yahweh" in the Old Testament. Thus, when the Church applies the title "Lord" to the Holy Spirit, she is saying that the Holy Spirit is truly God, co-equal with the Father and the Son.

According to St. Paul, "the Spirit brings life" (2 Cor. 3:6). Since it is the Holy Spirit who pours out charity in the hearts of the faithful (Gal. 4:6), he is the source of divine life in us. So in the Nicene Creed we proclaim our belief that the Holy Spirit is "the giver of life."

As we have seen, the Son proceeds from the Father alone who is the origin or principle of both the Son and the Holy Spirit. The idea of "procession" or "coming forth" in the inner divine life has its basis in a number of Scriptural texts. Jesus says of himself in John 8:42, "For I proceeded and came forth from God"; and he says of the Spirit that he "proceeds from the Father" (John15:26). In these texts Jesus is speaking not only of the external manifestations of the Spirit and his own Incarnation in time and space, but he is also referring to the internal, eternal origin of himself and the Holy Spirit.

Both Father and Son constitute one principle of the Holy Spirit because the Son, by virtue of his eternal generation from the Father, possesses everything that the Father possesses except the fatherhood. In John 16:15 Jesus says in testimony of this, "All that the Father has is mine." This means that he must be the principle, along with the Father, of the Holy Spirit.

Let me remind you that we previously spoke about the procession of the Son from the Father. There we said that the Son was "generated" from the Father. Thus there are two processions in the inner divine life of God: the procession of the Son from the Father which we call "generation," and the procession of the Holy Spirit from the Father and the Son as from one principle. Since the Holy Spirit is not "generated" by the Father and the Son, he is not to be called something like a second Son of God. Jesus Christ is the "only-begotten Son of God." So there is only one divine Son.

The Fathers of the Church invented a new word to designate the procession of the Holy Spirit. They called it "spiration" or "breathing forth." The word, of course, is related to "spirit" or "breath." The reason for this is that the Holy Spirit proceeds from the will or the mutual love of the Father and the Son. Hence he has a special relationship to love, which is an impulse or impelling of sorts. The connection between the Holy Spirit and love is brought out by St. Paul in Romans 5:5, "The charity of God is poured forth into our hearts by the Holy Spirit, who is given to us."

Both the Bible and Tradition teach us that the procession of the Son is related to God's knowing and the procession of the Holy Spirit is related to God's willing and loving. For this reason the Son is said to be the "wisdom" of God and the Holy Spirit is said to be the "love" or "gift" of God.

There is only one God and to God alone are due glory, worship and adoration. As we have seen, the Creed, however, proclaims faith in three distinct, not separate, Persons in God: Father, Son and Holy Spirit. We acknowledge God the Father as our Creator and so offer him our praise and adoration. God the Son, incarnate in Jesus of Nazareth, is our Redeemer. We worship him and show him homage—not only in our prayers, but especially in the Blessed Sacrament of the altar.

In the early history of the Church, the question arose about the nature and place of the Holy Spirit who spoke through the prophets, who was active in Jesus during his public life, who descended upon the Apostles at Pentecost and who manifested himself through many marvelous gifts imparted to those who believed in the Lord Jesus and had the hands of the Apostles laid upon their heads.

When theological reflection on Christian revelation began to develop in the third century and afterwards, there was some question as to the divinity and the personality of the Holy Spirit. In order to affirm both of these points the Nicene Creed states: "With the Father and the Son, he (the Holy Spirit) is worshipped and glorified." So, just as worship and glory are offered by Christians to the Father and the Son, so also are they with perfect right offered to the Holy Spirit. This means that the Holy Spirit is co-equal with the Father and the Son in divinity and majesty.

It follows then that just as the Father and the Son are divine Persons, subsisting in the one divine substance, so also is the Holy Spirit. One of the clearest indications of this truth in the New Testament is the missionary formula at the conclusion of St. Matthew's Gospel where the three Persons are mentioned and given the same level of dignity: "Go therefore and make disciples of all nations, baptizing them in the name of the Father and of the Son and of the Holy Spirit" (Matt. 28:19).

We say in the Creed that we "worship" and "glorify" the Holy Spirit. Worship frequently means "adoration" of God which can be expressed in many different ways: through prayer, sacrifice, solitude, penance. The main idea in adoration is that man, the weak creature, recognizes his creaturehood and therefore his total dependence on almighty God. When we "glorify" God, we praise and give expression to his infinite perfections such as his goodness, power and love. Thus worship and glory are offered to the Holy Spirit in the same sense as they are offered to the Father and the Son.

Thus a number of Catholic truths are expressed in the statement of the Creed. We are proclaiming that the Holy Spirit is truly God, since God alone can be worshipped and glorified by man. Likewise we are stating that the Holy Spirit is co-equal with the Father and the Son. He is the Third Person in the Blessed Trinity who has been revealed to us in the Scriptures, especially by the life and teaching of Jesus Christ. He manifested himself in the life of Jesus; Jesus imparted him to his Apostles and to the Church; he has been operative in the Church sanctifying and encouraging, since Pentecost Sunday.

With the Church we pray: "Come, Holy Spirit, and fill the hearts of the faithful."

The Nicene Creed also says of the Holy Spirit that "He spoke through the prophets." The reference is primarily to the prophets of the Old Testament, including such giants as Isaiah, Jeremiah, Ezekiel, Amos and Hosea.

In the Old Testament a prophet is not primarily one who predicts the future. The idea of a prophet as one who predicts future events is a popular conception that corresponds with only a part of the function of the true prophet. A prophet is simply someone, inspired by God, who speaks in the name of God and who expresses God's commands or his promises.

Certain traits distinguish the prophets of Israel. In the first place, a prophet is constituted by a divine call. This is evident in the call of Isaiah, Jeremiah and Ezekiel (see Isa. 6:5; Jer. 1:9; Ezek. 3:1 ff.). The prophet is always called by God for a religious purpose—he receives a divine mission. That mission is usually to proclaim the Word of God to Israel or to some specific individual, such as Nathan rebuking David for his adultery with Bathsheba (2 Sam. 12:1–15).

The true prophets encounter great trials and suffering in the process of bringing the will of God to their fellow men. Jeremiah, conscious of the responsibility of being a prophet, begged God to leave him in peace and to find someone else to do the prophesying (see Jer. 1). Under the kings in Israel and Judah the prophets were often executed (Jer. 2:30; 26:2–23). Thus Jesus was able to say: "O Jerusalem, Jerusalem, killing the prophets and stoning those who are sent to you...." (Matt. 23–37).

In the Old Testament "the Spirit of the Lord" descends on the prophet and he speaks. Thus there is a close association between the Holy Spirit and the human activity of speaking. The prophets counseled the community of Israel, they rebuked her; they denounced the kings and the wealthy oppressors of the poor; they spoke about the "Messiah"—the mysterious anointed king who would one day come to redeem Israel.

In the New Testament Jesus is vividly described in terms that indicate a Spirit-filled prophet who is mighty in word and deed.

Although he does not call himself a prophet explicitly, he is referred to by others a number of times as a great prophet from the Lord. The Holy Spirit is active in his conception (Luke 1:35; Matt. 1:20), leads him into the desert to be tempted (Luke 4:1), and directs him back to Nazareth, his home town, where he proclaims that the prophecy of Isaiah (61:1–2) is now fulfilled in his own person: "The Spirit of the Lord is upon me, because he has anointed me to preach good news to the poor" (Luke 4:18). And Jesus sends the Holy Spirit to each one of us when we pray with faith and especially when we receive him in Holy Communion.

All of this is perfectly expressed in the Creed at Mass: "I believe in the Holy Spirit, the Lord and Giver of life, who proceeds from the Father and the Son, who together with the Father and the Son is worshipped and glorified, who spoke through the prophets." Amen.

CREED: ARTICLE 9

"I Believe in the Holy Catholic Church, the Communion of Saints"

The Creed embodies our official profession of faith as Roman Catholics. The three major sections concern the Holy Trinity—Father, Son and Holy Spirit. In the final section we profess our faith in the Church, forgiveness of sins, resurrection of the body and eternal life. Let us now reflect on our faith in the Church: "I believe in the holy Catholic Church, the communion of saints."

If you think about it for a moment, it is truly astonishing that we say we believe in "the Church." Non-Catholic Christians do not look upon the Church as we do. For many of them, the Church is an historical "accident" not intended by Christ—something that just happened after the death of Jesus. They do not look upon the Church as a structured body, a hierarchical institution or a perfect society that was founded by Christ on Peter, the "rock," and intended to remain until the Second Coming of Jesus in glory.

For the Catholic, however, the Church is all of that and more. The Church is also the pilgrim People of God on its way to the glory of the Father; it is the Mystical Body of Christ—a <u>body</u> because it is structured, visible and historical, and <u>mystical</u> because it is animated by the Spirit of Jesus Christ; it is the Bride of Christ which he loves and for which he offered his life; it is a holy temple composed of many parts; it is a sacred community, held together by one faith and one Baptism, which operates through the seven sacraments given to her by her Founder.

No matter which image is used to describe the Church, none of them is completely adequate because the Church is a "mystery." This means that the total spiritual reality of the Church ultimately escapes the confines of human concepts and images. The principle which makes the Church possible in the first place is from above, for the Church is from God and transcends the capacity of the human mind fully to comprehend it.

In early Christian mosaics, the Church was often represented by Noah's ark, the idea being that just as Noah and his family were saved from the flood by the ark, so also the Church is the "ark" of salvation for us. Thus we find St. Cyprian in the third century saying that "outside the Church there is no salvation," an idea that has been repeated in Church documents since that time (see Vatican II, Constitution on the Church, 14). The formula was narrowly understood by Fr. Leonard Feeney in the late 1940s, but in clarifying the Church's position on the matter the Holy Office in 1949, in a letter that was approved by Pope Pius XII, explained that those who are in a state of invincible ignorance about the necessity of belonging to the Catholic Church can be saved if they have at least an <u>implicit desire</u> to enter the Church and if their hearts are informed with <u>perfect charity</u> (see DS 3866–73).

When we say that "I believe in the Church" we are making the Church an object of supernatural and divine faith. When we believe something by divine faith, this means that we accept it as true on the Word of God himself who has revealed it to us.

Thus the very existence of the Church, including her essential structure and her outstanding characteristics, has been revealed to us by Jesus Christ. Accordingly, we profess our belief in the one Church of Jesus Christ when we pray the Creed.

How do we know which church is the true church of Jesus Christ? Since the time of the early Church, bishops and theologians have designated four "marks" of the Church which are mentioned in the Nicene Creed which we say at each Sunday Mass: One, Holy, Catholic, and Apostolic.

So it is an article of Catholic faith that there is only one Church of Jesus Christ—the Church that he founded on Peter and the Apostles and that continues to this very moment only in the Roman Catholic Church. We profess this belief in the Nicene Creed when we say, "I believe in one Church."

In our experience, however, we encounter many Christian bodies that claim to be the true Church of Jesus Christ. It has been estimated that there are more than 20,000 versions of Protestantism. St. Paul said that we are "one body" in Christ, but our painful experience tells us that the body of Christ is divided into many. The causes of these divisions can be found through a careful historical analysis of the beginning of the various religious bodies.

Many Christian religions do not claim to be the one true Church of Jesus Christ. However, the Catholic Church has claimed at least since the time of St. Paul that "there is one body and one Spirit, just as you were called to the one hope that belongs to your call, one Lord, one faith, one baptism, one God and Father of us all" (Eph. 4:4–6). She claims to be, and we Catholic believe, that she is the one true Church.

When we say that the Catholic Church is "one" we are not only affirming that it is the only true Church of Jesus Christ, and therefore that all the other Christian bodies are defective in some way; we are also saying that the Church is undivided in itself, that it has internal and external unity. Internal or spiritual unity is achieved through the possession of the one Spirit of Christ that he poured out on his Church on Pentecost and continues to pour out on those who believe and receive the sacraments. External unity is attained through the unity of doctrine, worship and government. The Catholic Church is one in all three senses because it has a unified hierarchy that is in communion with the Pope, the successor St. Peter, and is subject to his universal authority or jurisdiction in the Church. Unity of faith, worship and leadership produce one Church.

Jesus founded one Church, not many churches, when he said "I will build my Church" on Peter, the rock (see Matt. 16:18). At the Last Supper he prayed, "that they may all be one even as thou, Father, art in me, and I in thee... so that the world may believe that thou hast sent me" (John 17:21). The unity of the Catholic Church has been a perpetual source of conversions in the past, since it is obvious to anyone who studies and meditates on the Jesus of the Gospels that he willed only one Church. He bequeathed unity and peace to us, not division and discord.

At this stage in history, no one knows how complete unity can be restored. Certainly it will never be accomplished by following the advice of some Catholic intellectuals who seem to be willing to sacrifice truth for the sake of unity. Unity must be based on truth, for unity based on error is no unity at all. We should pray for the unity of all Christians in one Church in the words of Our Lord, "that they may be one."

The second mark or note of the Church is that it is "holy." At its root "holiness" means the infinite fullness of the divine being, power and goodness that we are able to grasp in some way through normal human experience. It always remains mysterious to us and so it is ineffable, but at the same time it has a strange fascination. Theologians also speak of the "moral" holiness of God, which means his will, which essentially consists in his love—first of himself and then of all the creatures that he has produced out of nothingness.

Persons and things are said to be "holy" to the extent that they are dedicated to God, or close to him or related to him and his service in some way. So the notion of holiness belongs primarily to God and only secondarily to creatures.

The Church is the community of all those who have faith in Jesus Christ and possess his Spirit. It is a dogma of our Catholic faith that the Church herself is holy, since her holiness is professed in the Nicene Creed.

The Church is holy in her origin, her purpose, her means and the results she produces. She is holy in her origin since she was founded by Jesus Christ himself and was given the Holy Spirit as her animating principle. In fact, St. Paul says that Jesus is the head of the Church and the members constitute his Body—the Mystical Body of Christ. The Church is also holy in her purpose which is the glory of God and the sanctification and salvation of men.

Certain aspects of the holiness of the Church are visible to those who are willing to look and see. It is this "visible" holiness of the Church that is meant by the holy as a "mark" of the true Church of Jesus Christ.

The Church is holy in her fruits, that is, she is known from the holiness of those men and women who make full use of the means of grace and holiness put at their disposal by the Church. These are the "saints" of the Church, like St. Padre Pio and Bl. Mother Teresa. From her "fruits" she is seen to be holy and so holiness is one of the marks of the true Church of Jesus Christ.

The third "mark" of the true Church of Jesus Christ is that she must be "catholic," which means "universal." The Church founded by Jesus was called "catholic" in the second century by some of the early Fathers of the Church, such as St. Ignatius of Antioch and St. Polycarp. It began appearing in various creeds towards the end of the second century and has been in the Nicene Creed since the fourth century. So, that the true Church of Jesus Christ is "catholic" is an article of faith and is to be believed by all.

The universality of God's salvific will for all men was suggested in the Old Testament, but does not come to full fruition until God established a new and eternal covenant with man in Jesus Christ. St. Paul says that "God desires all men to be saved and to come to the knowledge of the truth" (1 Tim. 2:4). Before ascending into heaven, Jesus commanded his Apostles: "Go therefore and make disciples of all nations, baptizing them in the name of the Father and of the Son and of the Holy Spirit (Matt. 28:19; also Mark 16:15; Acts 1:8).

The catholicity of the Church has both an external and an internal dimension. *Externally*, it means that the Church is a unified body that authentically derives from Jesus Christ who founded her and is both basically and actually spread throughout the world. *Internally*, it means that the Church of Christ is endowed with all of the supernatural means (Gospel, grace, sacraments, hierarchy) necessary to effect the eternal salvation of all people at all times and in every land.

Since the time of the Apostles to the present day, the only Christian Church that claims to be "catholic" in the sense described is the Holy Roman Catholic Church. In fact, the notion of catholicity is so important that it is included in the very name of the Church. She is the parent Church that precedes all other Christian churches.

The apostolicity of the Church means the essential identity everywhere and since the time of her foundation with the Church of the Apostles. Thus the Church that has remained faithful to what the Apostles founded and bequeathed to their successors is by that very fact "apostolic." It follows also from this that such a Church is also the true Church of Jesus Christ since he is the "cornerstone." St. Paul says that the Church was "built on the foundation of the Apostles and prophets, Christ Jesus himself being the cornerstone" (Eph. 2:20).

The apostolicity of the Church is manifested in three ways: 1) apostolic origin, that is, the Church was founded by Christ on the Twelve Apostles and especially through them; 2) the apostolic doctrine, that is, the identity of faith with that preached by the Apostles; 3) the apostolic succession, that is, the uninterrupted chain of legitimate bishops who link the Church of the Apostles with the Church of today. Thus, today Pope Benedict XVI is the 265th successor of St. Peter. There is no other organization on this earth with a pedigree like that, going back uninterruptedly for 2000 years.

The only Church today that manifests the fullness of apostolicity is the Holy Roman Catholic Church. The Protestant churches lack apostolic origin, since they did not appear until the 16th century when they broke away from Catholic unity. They are also defective in the doctrine of the Apostles and they do not have the necessary apostolic succession.

The situation of the Eastern Orthodox churches is different. They do have the apostolic succession of their bishops, going back to the Apostles, but they are defective in some teachings and, especially, they have broken communion with the pope, who is the legitimate successor of St. Peter and the source of unity in the Church.

The Catholic Church claims to be "apostolic" in a unique sense that applies to her alone. She alone claims to possess, in the person of our Holy Father in Rome, the power of the keys that Our Lord promised to St. Peter and conferred on him (see Matt. 16:18–19). She has always acted in this confidence. This belief is emblazoned in marble wherever you look, both inside and outside, in St. Peter's Basilica in Rome.

The four notes of unity, sanctity, catholicity and apostolicity are not just hidden characteristics; they are external, recognizable marks of the true Church of Christ. Under Pope Pius IX the Holy Office declared: "The true Church of Christ, by virtue of divine authority, is constituted and is knowable by the four characteristics, which we confess in the Creed as an object of the faith" (DS 2888).

The Apostles' Creed here expands the notion of the Church and calls it "the communion of saints." This expression refers to the community of all the faithful in Christ—those on earth, those in purgatory and those in heaven. *Church* in this sense transcends the earthly limits of time and space and reaches into the non-temporal life with God.

The communion of saints is a vital fellowship between all the redeemed, on earth and in the next life; it is based on the common possession of the divine life of grace that comes to us through the risen Christ.

We can never thank God enough for calling us to be members of his one, holy, catholic and apostolic Church which is the communion of saints and the only ark of salvation.

CREED: ARTICLE 10

"I Believe in the Forgiveness of sins"

The tenth article of the Apostles' Creed is, "I believe in the forgiveness of sins." One of the greatest consolations found in being a member of the Catholic Church is the Sacrament of Penance in which and by which we can obtain the forgiveness of our sins no matter how serious they may be. God is infinite love, goodness and mercy so his mercy is greater than man's sinfulness, no matter what it might be. No sin is so great that God cannot or will not forgive it, provided that the sinner truly repents.

Jesus Christ, the Son of God and Second Person of the Blessed Trinity, became man and entered into this world of time and space to save each and every one of us from the Original Sin of Adam and also from our own personal sins. The name "Jesus" means "Savior." So Jesus saves us. What does he save us from? He saves us from sin and the power of evil. One of the main themes of the Bible is the reality of sin in human beings and its disastrous effects. We find this truth expressed again and again in Genesis, Exodus, Numbers and Judges. God reveals himself as the Holy One who is opposed to all sin. The reason and purpose of his revelation is to free man from sin, to sanctify him, and to bring him ultimately to heaven.

At Mass, when the priest consecrates the wine he says: "For this is the chalice of my Blood, of the New and Eternal Testament: The Mystery of Faith: which shall be shed for you and for many unto the remission of sins." Christ shed his blood for us and died for us for the remission of our sins.

When we pray the Apostles' Creed we say that we believe in "the forgiveness of sins." In the Nicene Creed which we say at Sunday Mass, we say: "I acknowledge one Baptism for the forgiveness of sins." Please notice that in the Sunday Creed we add faith in the power of Baptism to forgive sins. The first and total forgiveness of sins we receive is in Baptism which wipes away all sins and even the temporal punishment for them in purgatory. But Baptism does not change man's nature which has been partially corrupted by Original Sin; we still have what the theologians call "concupiscence" which in plain language means a tendency to sin, an attraction to sin, a tendency to assert oneself against the will of God as expressed in the Ten Commandments. In a time of temptation we all feel the urge to say, "I will not serve!" So Baptism does take away sins but it does not make man sinless. He retains his free will and so can rebel against God. Jesus instituted the Sacrament of Penance to provide a way of forgiveness for sins committed after Baptism. That is the situation we all find ourselves in. Accordingly, the Church urges us to make frequent use of the Sacrament and to go to confession on a regular basis. For some it is weekly, for others monthly, and for others once a year. That is a minimum.

How do we know that the Church has the power to forgive sins? The biblical basis is found in John 20:23. On Easter Sunday evening Jesus appeared to the disciples in the Upper Room in Jerusalem. He breathed on them and said to them: "Receive the Holy Spirit. If you forgive the sins of any, they are forgiven; if you retain the sins of any, they are retained." That power was passed on from the Apostles to the bishops and from the bishops to the priests of today. Also, it is the infallible teaching of the Church that Penance or Reconciliation is one of the Seven Sacraments instituted by Christ himself. Notice in John 20:23 that Jesus first breathes on them (spirit) and gives them the Holy Spirit before he gives them the power of forgiving sins. So there is a close connection between the Holy Spirit and the forgiveness of sins. That connection is made in the Apostles' Creed which says: "I believe in the Holy Spirit, the holy Catholic Church, the communion of saints, the forgiveness of sins" and so forth.

The main sources, therefore, of God's forgiveness of sins are found in Baptism and the Sacrament of Penance or Confession. Grave sins can also be forgiven by the Sacrament of the Anointing of the Sick (Extreme Unction), if the dying person is properly disposed by sorrow for his sins. Venial sins can be forgiven by the opening prayers of the Mass and a sincere recitation of the "Confiteor." So there are several ways in which we can obtain "the forgiveness of sins."

The power to forgive sins is often referred to as "the power of the keys." After his Resurrection, Christ sent his Apostles "so that repentance and forgiveness of sins should be preached in his name to all nations" (Luke 24:47). The CCC #981 quotes St. Augustine on this point: "[The Church] has received the keys of the Kingdom of heaven so that, in her, sins may be forgiven through Christ's blood and the Holy Spirit's action. In this Church, the soul dead through sin comes back to life in order to live with Christ, whose grace has saved us."

St. John Chrysostom said: "Priests have received from God a power that he has given neither to angels nor to archangels.... God above confirms what priests do here below" (CCC #983). Let me quote St. Augustine again: "Were there no forgiveness of sins in the Church, there would be no hope of life to come or eternal liberation. Let us thank God who has given his Church such a gift" (CCC #983). Today let us thank God for the gift of the Sacrament of Penance—for Confession. It is a good idea, and helpful for avoiding serious sin, to make it a habit to go to confession regularly, at least once a month. For, in Confession you receive forgiveness of your sins; you receive an increase of grace to help you to avoid sins; you can also receive some spiritual advice from the priest.

The saints advocate frequent Confession. St. Francis Borgia, head of the Jesuit Order in the 17th century, went to confession every day. Also the Jesuit theologian, Fr. John Hardon, author of many books on the faith, and a personal friend, went to confession every day. Some of his followers and admirers have introduced his cause for beatification because he was such a holy man. Each one here should say to himself: "I believe in the Holy Spirit, the holy Catholic Church, the communion of saints, and the forgiveness of sins." God bless you.

CREED: ARTICLE 11

"I Believe in the Resurrection of the Dead"

The Apostles' Creed concludes by proclaiming faith in the resurrection of the dead and life everlasting: "I believe in the resurrection of the dead." These are happy truths that urge us to shout for joy. Death is not the final chapter in the life of one who dies in Christ, in the state of sanctifying grace. Death is swallowed up in the victory of everlasting life.

Resurrection means the return of a dead man to life. But in the resurrection on the last day, when the soul is reunited to the body, life will be different from what it is now. It will be the glorious life that we see in the resurrected Jesus in the Gospels. He appears and disappears at will; he passes through walls; he cannot suffer and is immortal. It is hard for us to imagine that type of life.

Some years ago on a trip to Italy I visited the cathedral in the city of Orvieto—about fifty miles north of Rome. In a side chapel there is a huge mural painting of the resurrection. It shows people climbing up out of the ground in various stages of the soul being reunited to the body. That painting made a deep impression on me.

In the Old Testament there was a gradual development of the belief in the resurrection which reached its high point in the prophet Daniel and in 2 Maccabees in the 2nd century B.C. In New Testament times the idea was embraced by the Pharisees but rejected by the Sadducees—those constant opponents of Jesus. They were crass materialists who believed only in the here and now. In our own day by logical necessity all rationalists, materialists and atheists must, if they are true to their own principles, reject the notion of resurrection of the dead as absurd. They must reject it because it is so clearly beyond all human powers. Thus, if there is a resurrection, there must be a God who effects it, and they will not admit that.

Jesus clearly taught the resurrection of the dead in the Gospels. This doctrine is a favorite theme of St. John and also of St. Paul who gives it extensive treatment in 1 Corinthians 15:12–14: "How can some of you say that there is no resurrection of the dead? But if there is no resurrection of the dead, then Christ has not been raised; if Christ has not been raised, then our preaching is in vain and your faith is in vain.... But in fact Christ has been raised from the dead, the first fruits of those who have fallen asleep."

The "resurrection of the dead" professed in the Creed will take place at the end of the world—a time, unknown to anyone except the Father (Mark 13:32), when this whole changing world as we know it will be transformed by the power of God into something completely new. That is the moment when Jesus will come again in his glory and will judge the living and the dead. This event is also known as the "Parousia" of the Lord and "the Second Coming."

If the "resurrection" means the return to life of the dead, what kind of life will it be? It will be a life of supreme joy and happiness for those who have died in the love of God and are saved. A point to stress here is that the joy of the saved affects not only the soul, but the whole person of body and soul. For, at the resurrection, the soul will be reunited to the body which will share in and reflect the glory of the soul. Also, it is a defined teaching of the Fourth Lateran Council (1215) that the dead will rise with the same body they had on earth. Since all of the matter in our bodies changes about every five years, obviously we will not have exactly the same matter or molecules that we had in time, but we will look the same and will retain our sexual differentiation.

How many of us really "expect" or "look forward to" the resurrection? The word in the Creed implies a certain longing in the Christian for the end of the world and the Second coming of Christ—a time when all suffering, evil and death will be wiped away for the redeemed.

Our concern here is primarily with the saved, but it is also Catholic teaching that "all" the dead will rise again—both the saved and the damned. This teaching is based on the clear words of Jesus (Matt. 10:28; John 5:29). Thus the damned will suffer in hell both in soul and in body.

Jesus himself is the "first fruits" from the dead, as St. Paul said. Our Blessed Mother has also been assumed body and soul into heaven. Jesus set the pattern for her and for all of us. This means that we will be transformed into a glory similar to his.

On this point St. Paul says in 1 Cor. 15:35–37 ff.): "But someone will ask, 'How are the dead raised? With what sort of body do they come?' You foolish man! What you sow does not come to life unless it dies. And what you sow is not the body which is to be, but a bare kernel.... What is sown is perishable, what is raised is imperishable.... The dead will be raised imperishable.... For this perishable nature must put on the imperishable, and this mortal nature must put on immortality."

In the past theologians have distinguished four qualities of resurrected bodies. They are: 1) the incapability of suffering and dying; 2) the spiritualization of the body so that it is no longer subject to the laws of nature as it now is; 3) agility, or the capability of the body to obey the soul with greatest ease and speed of movement; 4) perfection of radiance and beauty. In this regard St. Paul, who had a mystical vision of heaven, said: "Eye has not seen, nor ear heard, nor the heart of man conceived, what God has prepared for those who love him" (1 Cor. 2:9).

To unbelievers the resurrection of the dead is foolishness. But to those of us who believe in God and in his infallible Word, the resurrection of Jesus, who said "I am the Resurrection and the life" (John 11:25), is the pledge of our own personal resurrection and liberation from the iron jaws of death and corruption.

On Easter Sunday we celebrate each year the resurrection of Jesus from the dead, which is the pledge or promise of our own resurrection. The Church urges us to rejoice, using the words of the Psalmist in the Gradual (118:24), "This is the day the Lord has made; let us rejoice and be glad in it." We rejoice in the truth of the resurrection which is the foundation of our Christian hope of eternal life. This is an essential part of the "Good News" of salvation in Jesus Christ. God bless you.

CREED: ARTICLE 12

"I Believe in Life Everlasting"

The Creed concludes with a strong note of hope—hope for the resurrection of the dead and "life everlasting." In this final sermon on the Creed we will reflect on the meaning of "everlasting life" or "eternal life."

From our own experience we all know what life is. It is the supreme good in this world—something we strive to preserve at all cost. Men and women will give up their wealth and undergo the most painful operations and treatments in order to sustain their lives a few more months or years. And constantly we live in the shadow of death—the all consuming, rapacious, inescapable jaws that eventually devour each one of us.

From physical death, and the personal disintegration that it connotes, we hope to escape by entering into eternal life. By his death and Resurrection Jesus was victorious over death. All those who enter into his life-death-Resurrection by faith, by Baptism and by the exercise of the theological virtues of faith, hope and charity, are summoned by the Father to be participators with Christ in the eternal kingdom.

By faith we know that in addition to our material-biological life on earth there is another, higher life of grace that is open to all who believe in the Father, in Jesus Christ his only Son, and in the Holy Spirit. The supernatural life of grace is an unmerited, total gift of God which begins in this life by faith and Baptism and is brought to completion in "the world to come" when the veils of this flesh are removed so that we can see God as he is, face to face.

Our infallible Catholic faith teaches us that our life does not cease at death. In the Preface of the Mass for the Dead the Church prays that in death life is not extinguished but only changed into a new, permanent, glorious kind of life.

We pray in the Creed that we are looking for life everlasting. There are many scriptural overtones in this expression. We know from our faith that one day God will destroy the present world. This means that one day there will be an end to conception, birth, growth and death. The New Testament writers speak of the "new heaven and the new earth" that God is going to fashion. What this new heaven and earth will be like and how God will accomplish his plan, he has not seen fit to reveal to us.

God's purpose in creating the universe, the human race and each human person, is that we might share in his abundant life. That is the end that he intends for each and every one of us. Our life on this earth is a painful pilgrimage on our way towards eternal life with God. St. Teresa of Avila, a great mystic and a great woman, said that this life is like spending a night in a bad inn or, as we would now say, in a lousy motel.

St. Paul tells us that God desires that all men be saved and that all come to a knowledge of the truth (1 Tim. 2:4). However, in order to attain the permanent divine life that he had in store for us, he demands that we freely love him in return for his many kindnesses to us. And the way we show that we love God is by keeping his commandments (John 14:15). He created us without consulting us, but he will not save us without our free cooperation.

Accordingly, we see that there is a well thought out plan in the Creed: it moves from the Father, to the Son, to the Holy Spirit, to the Church and finally to the "last things"—especially the resurrection and life everlasting.

At the end of this life there are two possibilities for each person: 1) eternal happiness with God in heaven, or 2) eternal punishment and misery in hell for those who die without the grace of God and as his enemies.

At death each person is judged immediately. If those who are destined for heaven have to make satisfaction for sins committed, they are sent to purgatory for a time to make proper restitution for the sins they have committed. If the person's soul is perfectly clean and filled with love of God, that person will go immediately to heaven to be with the angels and saints. This happens to martyrs for the faith and to those who die immediately after Baptism. "Heaven is the ultimate end and fulfillment of the deepest human longings, the state of supreme, definitive happiness" (see CCC #1024). Those who die in the state of mortal sin are sent immediately to hell. All of these points were clearly stated and defined by Pope Benedict XII in 1336 (*Benedictus Deus*) and are explained in detail in the *Catechism of the Catholic Church*.

These truths about the resurrection of the body and everlasting life presuppose, of course, the sad and painful reality of death, from which no one is excused. The key to all of this is to die the right way, and that means to die "in Christ," to die in the state of sanctifying grace which we received at our Baptism and nourished throughout our life by frequent reception of the Sacraments and the practice of love of God and love of neighbor.

The Christian who unites his own death to that of Jesus views it as a step towards him and an entrance into everlasting life. When the Church for the last time speaks Christ's words of pardon and absolution over the dying Christian, seals him for the last time with a strengthening anointing, and gives him Christ in viaticum as nourishment for the journey, she speaks with gentle assurance:

"Go forth Christian soul, from this world
In the name of God the almighty Father,
who created you,
in the name of Jesus Christ, the Son of the living God,
who suffered for you,
in the name of the Holy Spirit,
who was poured out upon you.
Go forth, faithful Christian!

May you live in peace this day,
May your home be with God in Zion,
With Mary, the virgin Mother of God,
With Joseph, with all the angels and saints.

May your return to [your creator]
Who formed you from the dust of the earth.
May holy Mary, the angels, and all the saints
Come to meet you as you go forth from this life...
May you see your Redeemer face to face." (CCC #1020)

These are some of the thoughts we might entertain when we say, "I believe in life everlasting." God bless you.

SACRAMENT 1: BAPTISM

Today I want to speak to you about the Sacrament of Baptism which makes us members of the Church so that we can receive the other six Sacraments. Baptism is the entrance, the door, the gate through which we enter into the kingdom of God and become his adopted children with the right of inheritance of eternal glory forever in heaven. So Baptism is one of the most important events in the life of each one of us.

We should think of Baptism primarily of adults, not of children. In the early Church most of the newly baptized were adults, not children. The Baptism of children is a separate question which we will not deal with here. I will try to get across to you the full meaning of Baptism for an adult who freely makes an act of faith in Jesus Christ and requests Baptism. All the Sacraments are personal, free acts and are not valid if one does not have the right intention. Christian life and Christian culture depend on and are the result of Baptism into the life of Christ.

The *Roman Catechism* defines Baptism as the sacrament of regeneration through water in the word. A sacrament is a visible sign of invisible grace instituted by Christ. Let us now reflect on each part of the definition of Baptism in order to get a clear idea of what it is. The word "baptism" comes from a Greek word which means to plunge or to dip something or someone into water. It means to purify or to cleanse with water, since water is our principal purifying agent. Baptism for the repentance of sins, and now with a spiritual meaning, was practiced by St. John the Baptist and Jesus himself was baptized by John as a sign of his humility and identity with us, even though he is absolutely sinless.

The basic notion in Baptism is spiritual regeneration. In the early Church it was done by immersion in the water three times, while invoking the name of the Father and the Son and the Holy Spirit. Jesus himself instituted the Sacrament of Baptism. While speaking to Nicodemus, he said: "I solemnly assure you, unless a man is born again of water and the Spirit, he cannot enter into the kingdom of God" (John 3:5). Before his Ascension Jesus commanded his disciples: "All power in heaven and on earth has been given to me. Go, therefore, and make disciples of all nations, baptizing them in the name of the Father, and of the Son, and of the Holy Spirit..." (Matt. 28:18–20). And Jesus says in St. Mark on the same point: "Go to every part of the world and proclaim the gospel.... Those who believe it and receive baptism will be saved; those who do not believe will be condemned" (16:16). Notice here the important connection between faith and baptism. A consequence of this is that Baptism, in water or blood or desire, is necessary for anyone to be saved and to reach heaven. We know that God desires the salvation of all his children (1 Tim. 2:4), but how he accomplishes this with those who do not know about Christ and Baptism, is a secret hidden from us, since God has not revealed to us how he deals with them.

On the first Pentecost and in his first sermon, St. Peter said in Jerusalem: "Repent and be baptized every one of you in the name of Jesus Christ for the forgiveness of your sins; and you will receive the gift of the Holy Spirit" (Acts 2:38). By Baptism we are made children of God and heirs of heaven. We are made participators in the divine life by means of sanctifying grace which is poured into our souls. By Baptism we are also incorporated into the body of Christ which is the Church. We become members of the holy community of saints which is animated by the Holy Spirit and whose head is Christ himself.

The Fathers of the Church saw many symbols or hints of Christian Baptism in the Old Testament. Some of those symbols are: the hovering of the Spirit of God over the primitive waters in Genesis 1, the flood in the time of Noah, the march of the people of God on dry ground through the Red Sea. The same water that saved the Chosen People also destroyed the army of the Egyptians.

Baptism is like a new birth. As St. Paul says, we become "new creatures" through faith and Baptism. Here we are talking about a "spiritual birth" to the supernatural life of grace. "The different effects of Baptism are signified by the perceptible elements of the sacramental rite. Immersion in water signifies not only death [to sin] and purification, but also regeneration and renewal. Thus the two principal effects of Baptism are purification from sins and regeneration or new birth in the Holy Spirit" (see CCC 1262).

PURIFICATION: One of the marvelous effects of Baptism is that it takes away Original Sin, inherited from Adam, and all personal mortal and venial sins. Not only that, it also takes away the temporal punishment due to personal sins in purgatory. So if a person dies after being baptized, he or she goes directly to heaven. The white cloth at Baptism symbolizes this purity of soul of the one just baptized.

REGENERATION OR NEW BIRTH: Baptism makes one "a new creature," an adopted son of God, who has become a "partaker of the divine nature," member of Christ and co-heir with him, and a temple of the Holy Spirit (see CCC 1265). The Most Holy Trinity gives the baptized sanctifying grace—the grace of JUSTIFICATION:

> —enabling them to believe in God, to hope in him, and to love him through the three theological virtues;
> —giving them the power to live and act under the prompting of the Holy Spirit through the seven gifts of the Holy Spirit;
> —allowing them to grow in goodness through the moral virtues. Thus the whole organism of the Christian supernatural life has its roots in Baptism.

Baptism also makes us members of the Body of Christ. Therefore, as members of the Church, we are members of one another. Baptism also seals the Christian with an indelible spiritual mark or character, which can never be lost. So Baptism can be received only once – it cannot be repeated like Penance and the Eucharist. Baptism entitles one to receive the other Sacraments and entitles one to share in the priestly office of Christ to offer sacrifice to God along with the priest at Mass.

Baptism is the entrance, the gate to the Super Highway that leads to heaven and eternal happiness. It gives us the right to travel on that road and the right to assistance along the way with the other six Sacraments. There is only one highway going to heaven and that is the Catholic Church and her Seven Sacraments. We are here on this earth for a few years to work out our salvation. The end for which God made us is eternal happiness with him in heaven forever. He has given us the means to get there, but we must freely accept them and abide by his rules found in human nature and in his revelation which is preserved and proclaimed by the Catholic Church.

When you reflect like this on Baptism you realize what a great gift it is from God. He is our Redeemer, our Savior and our eternal happiness because he is love, and because he invites us to share in his nature and his love by faith and Baptism. Our major goal in life should be to live in accordance with the meaning of our Baptism—to preserve the grace of Baptism. Fidelity to one's Baptism, and perseverance in virtue, means that we are sure to reach the end for which we were created, that is, the face to face vision of God in an embrace of love that will never end. Then the human heart will be fully satisfied.

SACRAMENT 2: CONFIRMATION

Closely related to Baptism is the Sacrament of Confirmation, which is one of the three sacraments of initiation, that is, when an adult enters the Church, he or she is baptized, confirmed and receives Our Lord in Holy Communion. In the present practice of the Church Confirmation is usually conferred on boys and girls in early adolescence.

The word "confirmation" itself means "strengthening." So Confirmation is the sacrament of spiritual strengthening through a special conferral of the Holy Spirit for those who have already received spiritual regeneration in Baptism. It is one of the seven sacraments of the Church instituted by Christ—it is a sign that signifies divine grace and also confers it infallibly.

In the order of nature we distinguish between birth and growth or maturity. So also in the supernatural order there is a difference between spiritual rebirth (Baptism) and spiritual maturity (Confirmation). In Baptism we receive the Holy Spirit in a beginning way, like taking the first bite of a sandwich or a meal, with much more to come later. Confirmation is the perfection of Baptism, that is, it strengthens us to stand up for Christ, to be proud of our faith, and to explain it to others when we have the opportunity. That is what happened to the Apostles: On Easter Sunday our Lord breathed on them and said, "Receive the Holy Spirit. Whose sins you forgive shall be forgiven...." But fifty days later, on Pentecost Sunday, they received the fullness of the Holy Spirit and suddenly became bold preachers of faith in Jesus Christ—the Good News of salvation in Christ.

The Rite or Liturgy of the Sacrament consists in the anointing on the forehead with a special oil consecrated by the local bishop usually on Holy Thursday. It is called "Chrism" which is an aromatic oil composed of olive oil and a perfume called "balsam." The symbolism of the aroma is the fragrance of Christ, that is, giving good example to others of the truth and goodness of the

Christian faith. The bishop puts his right hand on the head of the one being confirmed and while anointing the forehead says, "Be sealed with the gift of the Holy Spirit." Then he touches his cheek with his hand as a sign that the confirmed Christian must be ready to suffer persecution for the sake of Christ.

Those who are confirmed are supposed to know the basics of the Catholic faith as found in the catechism, that is, the Creed, the Sacraments, the Ten Commandments, and a few basic prayers like the Our Father, Hail Mary, and the acts of faith, hope, charity and contrition. The bishop usually will ask the one being confirmed some questions about the catechism.

In the Acts of the Apostles we see how the Apostles were changed on Pentecost when they received the fullness of the Holy Spirit. Confirmation also brings an increase and a deepening of our baptismal grace. Here are some of the things it does for us:

a. It roots us more deeply in the divine sonship which makes us cry, "Abba, Father";
b. It unites us more closely to Christ;
c. It increases the seven gifts of the Holy Spirit in us;
d. It makes our membership in the Church more perfect;
e. It gives us special strength to spread and defend the faith by word and action as true witnesses of Christ, to confess the name of Christ boldly, and never to be ashamed of the Cross of Jesus Christ. (See CCC 1303)

Like Baptism and Holy Orders, Confirmation can be given only once, because it imprints an indelible mark or character on the soul. This is a sign that Jesus has marked the Christian with the seal of his Holy Spirit so that he may be his witness. Here is what the Catechism says (CCC 1316): "Confirmation perfects Baptismal grace; it is the sacrament which gives the Holy Spirit in order to root us more deeply in the divine filiation, incorporate us more firmly into Christ, strengthen our bond with the Church, associate us more closely with her mission, and help us to bear witness to the Christian faith in words accompanied by deeds."

Confirmation is not necessary for salvation, as is Baptism, but the Church urges all Catholics to receive the Sacrament because of the extra graces it confers on us to help us to resist temptations, control our passions, and grow in virtue. So it is not possible to attain the fullness of the Christian life without the help of the Sacrament of Confirmation.

If anyone here today, listening to this sermon on Confirmation, has not been confirmed, then I urge you to get in touch with your pastor and make arrangements to be confirmed at the first opportunity. Confirmation has been called "The Sacrament of Christian Maturity." In the early Church the Holy Spirit was communicated by the imposition of hands; later on the anointing of oil was added because we are followers of Christ who is "the Anointed One" since that is what the word "Christ" means. So we read in the Acts of the Apostles (8:14–17): "Now when the apostles in Jerusalem heard that Samaria had received the word of God, they sent to them Peter and John, who came down and prayed for them that they might receive the Holy Spirit; for it had not yet fallen on any of them, but they had only been baptized in the name of the Lord Jesus. Then they laid their hands on them, and they received the Holy Spirit."

The Sacrament of Confirmation strengthens us in the faith and makes us better Catholics. We are all weak and need whatever spiritual aids we can get. The Lord Jesus offers us special strengthening of the Holy Spirit in the Sacrament of Confirmation so we can grow in virtue and the love of God. Because of that we can call it "The Sacrament of Christian Maturity."

SACRAMENT 3: HOLY EUCHARIST

We have considered Baptism and Confirmation. Today I propose to speak to you about the Holy Eucharist, which is the third "sacrament of initiation," that is, initiation into the Church which is the Body of Christ. Most Catholics now receive Holy Communion every Sunday and every time they attend Mass. It is an essential part of our holy Catholic faith. It is essential because the consecrated host contains, under the appearances of bread and wine, the body, Blood, Soul and Divinity of our Lord Jesus Christ, who is the Second Person in the Blessed Trinity, and God Almighty, the Creator of heaven and earth and my Creator.

An encounter like this, with our Creator and Redeemer, is something very important in our lives. It puts us in personal contact with our Creator; it brings us closer to God and is a pledge or promise of eternal life with God after our death if we remain faithful to him. So receiving Holy Communion should be a deeply personal event; interior acts of faith, hope and love should accompany the exterior act of taking Holy Communion. We must avoid being casual about Holy Communion, or receiving it merely out of habit with no interior acts of love.

Let us reflect briefly on what the Holy Eucharist is. The word itself is derived from the Greek word which means "thanksgiving." Because Jesus offered a prayer of thanksgiving when he consecrated the bread and wine at the Last Supper, the word has always been connected with the sacrament of the Lord's Supper. The Eucharist is that sacrament of the New Law in which Christ, under the forms of bread and wine, is really, truly and substantially present—Body, Blood, soul and divinity—in order to offer himself in an unbloody manner to the Heavenly Father, and to give himself to the faithful as nourishment for their souls. Hints or foreshadowings of the Eucharist are found in the Old Testament: for example, the "tree of life" in the Garden of Eden, the miraculous manna in the desert that nourished the Israelites in the wilderness for 40 years, the various sacrifices of the OT, especially that of the Paschal Lamb.

And in the New Testament we have changing of water into wine at the wedding feast of Cana, the multiplication of the five loaves of bread to feed 5000 people, and Jesus' sermon in John 6 in which he says that he is "the bread of life." The Eucharist enjoys a certain preeminence among the sacraments. They are instruments or channels of grace, but the Eucharist actually contains Jesus within itself who is the source of all grace. The other sacraments are all ordered to the Eucharist and they are usually followed by the reception of Holy Communion.

Belief in the Mass and the Eucharist is what, more than anything else, distinguishes us Catholics. We Catholics have a treasure here which is infinite. No effort should be spared to try to understand it better and to appreciate it more. For the Eucharist is a visible sign of God's love for us. In fact, it is "a sacrament of love in which Christ is eaten, the mind is filled with grace, and a pledge is given to us of future glory."

A fundamental point regarding the Eucharist is what is known as "the Real Presence." This means that the glorified Christ, now in heaven, is really, truly and physically present in the Eucharist under the appearances of bread and wine. This amazing transformation takes place as the result of the words of consecration, spoken by a validly ordained priest, when he says: "This is my Body" and "This is the cup of my Blood." Instantly, Jesus Christ, true God and true man, becomes actually present. The Church teaches us that the substance of the bread and wine are changed into the substance of the Body and Blood of Jesus Christ, but the bread and wine still look the same. What is called the accidentals remain the same—color, shape, size, taste, smell—but the reality has changed. The Church calls this marvelous change "transubstantiation." That is a big word, with Latin roots, which means a change of substance.

A priest friend of mine, a scientist, told me once that Albert Einstein was fascinated by the Catholic doctrine of transubstantiation. We say that Jesus is "really present" in the Eucharist.

"Presence" is one of those basic realities that we all know, but which is difficult to define. Basically it means "being in front of"; when it is said of persons, often it has the added meaning of "being for" or "being with," in the sense of accompanying someone. We are present to our relatives and friends. God is present to us in many ways, because he is infinite and is everywhere. By his conserving power he is present in all of creation; he is present in the souls of the just by his sanctifying grace; he is present in his Church which is the Mystical Body of Christ; he is present in priests by reason of their ordination; he is present in his word as contained in the Bible and preached during Mass. But Jesus' presence in the Holy Eucharist is a different kind of presence. Here, by the almighty power of God, a stupendous miracle has taken place, namely, the substance and reality of bread and wine are changed into the substance and reality of the Body and Blood of the glorified Christ who is now seated at the right hand of the Father in heaven. Therefore, since Jesus Christ is God, and God is worthy of adoration, it follows that the Lord, truly and personally present under the appearances of bread and wine, is worthy of adoration in the Holy Eucharist. For this reason the Church surrounds the Mass and the Eucharist with various gestures of adoration, such as incense, bows, genuflections, silence, formal liturgical vestments, and so forth.

The altar with the tabernacle on it which contains the Eucharist or Blessed Sacrament is the central focus point of a Catholic Church. The vigil light burns constantly as a reminder of the Real Presence. People visit Catholic churches and chapels to pray at all times because they know Jesus is present there. In this sense, a Catholic church is essentially different from a Protestant church where there is no Blessed Sacrament and no vigil light.

The principal fruit of receiving Holy Communion is an intimate union with Christ Jesus. As Jesus said in John 6:57, "As the living Father sent me, and I live because of the Father, so he who eats me will live because of me." What material food produces in our bodily life, Holy Communion wonderfully achieves in our spiritual life—it is nourishment for our soul so that we can grow in love of God. Also, the Eucharist cannot unite us to Christ without at the same time cleansing us from past sins and preserving us from future sins. As spiritual nourishment, it increases charity which helps to preserve us from future mortal sins.

In an ancient prayer the Church acclaims the mystery of the Eucharist: "O sacred banquet in which Christ is received as food, the memory of the Passion is renewed, the soul is filled with grace and a pledge of the life to come is given to us." [CCC 1402] There is no surer pledge or clearer sign of hope for eternal life than the Eucharist. Every time this mystery is celebrated, "the work of our redemption is carried on" and we "break the one bread that provides the medicine of immortality, the antidote for death, and the food that makes us live for ever in Jesus Christ." [CCC1405]

O Sacrament most holy, O Sacrament divine, all praise and all thanksgiving be every moment thine. Amen.

SACRAMENT 4: PENANCE

Baptism, Confirmation and Eucharist are called the sacraments of "initiation" into the life of grace and union with God. Penance and the Anointing of the Sick are called the sacraments of healing because they restore grace that is lost through the commission of a mortal sin which separates one from God and makes one deserving of hell. They also confer healing and an increase of grace on those who make a confession of devotion. Since Vatican II we have seen a dramatic decline in the numbers of Catholics who make regular use of the Sacrament of Penance. Now we have the anomalous situation in which most Catholics receive Communion at Sunday Mass, but rarely or never confess their sins to a priest in confession. This morning I propose to explain the Church's understanding of Penance—what it is, what it does for us, and why it is important.

This sacrament is called "penance" or "confession" or more recently, "reconciliation." It is the sacrament instituted by Christ by which sins committed after Baptism are forgiven through the absolution of the priest in confession. In his mercy Christ our Lord instituted Penance so that those who, through human weakness, fall into mortal sin might have a way to escape from their sin and return home to the grace and love of God. Ideally, the baptized Christian should never commit a mortal sin, but since people are weak and open to temptation, many do fall—some rarely and some often.

Penance is like a life preserver on the Ship of Salvation that is thrown to those who have fallen overboard into the sea of sin. If we were all perfect saints, there would be no need for Penance, but as a matter of fact we are all sinners, except for our Lord and his Blessed Mother. Jesus instituted this sacrament when he gave the power of binding and loosing to Peter (Matt. 16) and when he breathed on the Apostles on Easter Sunday and said to them, "Whose sins you shall forgive, they are forgiven, and whose sins you shall retain, they are retained" (John 20:23). The Catholic Church has always understood that bishops and priests have the power of absolving from sins in this sacrament.

In order to make a valid confession, the sinner must do three things:

1) He must have CONTRITION in his heart, that is, he must be sorry for his sins. Contrition is sorrow of the soul and detestation for the sin committed, together with the resolution not to sin again. Perfect Contrition means that the motive of sorrow is love of God and sorrow for having offended him; Imperfect Contrition means that the motive for sorrow is fear of God and fear of punishment in hell. Perfect Contrition is best, but imperfect contrition is sufficient for making a good confession and receiving forgiveness of one's sins. Without at least imperfect contrition on the part of the penitent, the confession is invalid and his sins are not forgiven.

2) The sinner must CONFESS his sins to a priest. All certain mortal sins must be confessed. Venial sins are optional, but the Church urges us to mention them also in confession. Sorrow for them helps us to grow in grace and holiness.

3) SATISFACTION: This means that the penitent must do the penance imposed by the priest, such as certain prayers, or fasting, or other good works. By reason of their ordination, priests have the power to absolve from serious sins, with a few exceptions of sins reserved to the bishop or the Pope, such as an attempt on the life of the Pope or consecrating bishops without the approval of the Pope. The role of the priest is like that of a judge—he must know the state of the soul of the one going to confession. That is why the penitent must say when his last confession took place, and tell the priest all of his or her mortal sins since the last confession. When the priest has that information, he can give the penitent some advice and also can give a suitable penance. The purpose of confession is the forgiveness of

sins, not psychological counseling. The priest can give the penitent some spiritual advice on how to avoid certain sins, but he is not a psychologist or psychiatrist. If the penitent needs that kind of help, it should be sought outside of the sacrament of Penance. Sometimes during a confession, a priest will recommend to the penitent that he or she seek psychological help.

Mortal sin, like fornication or adultery or serious theft, separates one from God. Mortal sin involves two things: 1) the guilt of the sin, and 2) the punishment that God metes out to the sinner—either in this life or in the next life. When a person makes a good confession and receives absolution from the priest, the guilt of the sin is forgiven by God and the person is restored to sanctifying grace. Some of the punishment is remitted by performing the penance imposed by the confessor. Punishment that is not absolved in this life, must be endured in purgatory when one dies.

Mortal sin, and the guilt that flows from it, causes a great burden on the soul. In his great mercy God has provided us with the Sacrament of Penance so we can be freed from the burden of sin and return to his friendship. The common result of making a good confession is that the penitent experiences a deep sense of joy and peace that God has forgiven him and that he is now once again on the way to heaven to find the happiness that he earnestly desires. It is like taking a great weight off his shoulders. In addition to his peace of soul, the penitent is now reconciled with God and reconciled with the Church as "a living member" of the Church.

As we learned in the catechism, man was created to know, love and serve God in this life and to be happy with him forever in the next life. Mortal sin is the greatest evil in the world because it causes the loss of sanctifying grace, separates one from God and establishes an impenetrable wall or chasm between man and God, which only God can remove. The Sacrament of Penance removes that wall or chasm, restores sanctifying grace and puts us once again in personal contact with God who is the source of all life and goodness and beauty.

Penance has been called a "second conversion" after Baptism. St. Peter's conversion after he had denied Jesus three times bears witness to this. Jesus' look of infinite mercy drew tears of repentance from Peter and, after the Lord's resurrection, a threefold affirmation of love for him. If Judas had repented, Jesus would have forgiven him and he would have been saved. St. Ambrose says of the two conversions that, in the Church, "there are water and tears: the water of Baptism and the tears of repentance." (CCC 1429)

Let us thank our Lord for the great gift of the Sacrament of Penance, the Sacrament of Forgiveness. It is another sign of his infinite love for us, his compassion for our weakness and his mercy. Let us resolve to go to confession on a regular basis so that we can receive his mercy and his grace that help us to grow in love and union with God. Every year the Church urges us to make a good confession during the time of Lent.

SACRAMENT 5: ANOINTING OF THE SICK

In recent weeks we have been considering the Sacraments which are efficacious visible signs of invisible grace established by Christ our Lord as an essential part of his Church. The supernatural grace of Christ, which makes us children of God and heirs of heaven, is our most precious possession. The main channels of grace are the seven sacraments. Today I would like to offer you a few observations on the sacrament we receive in a serious sickness or at the end of life—the Anointing of the Sick, which used to be called "Extreme Unction." That is, the last anointing before death and appearing before Christ as our Eternal Judge. Given our weakness and our sins, that is a frightful thought. The Christian desires to appear before him in the state of sanctifying grace and cleansed of all sins and the punishment due to those sins. In his mercy, Christ has given us a sacrament that strengthens us in sickness and prepares us to meet our God if God calls us to himself—the Anointing of the Sick.

We are all by nature mortal. That means that we are doomed to die at some time in the future. It applies to all—rich and poor, men and women, powerful and homeless. There is no escape. Every ancestor going back to Adam has gone through the process of suffering and death. Of course, Jesus rose from the dead, but only after he had suffered a painful death. In order to help us to meet death with courage, hope and peace of mind, Jesus gave us the Sacrament of Anointing of the Sick.

The Council of Trent called it the *sacramentum exeuntium*, that is, the sacrament of those passing over from this life to eternity. Our Christian life begins with Baptism; it is perfected by Confirmation and nourished by the Eucharist. If grace is lost by mortal sin, it is restored by Penance. Life is crowned, as it were, by the Anointing of the Sick which completes the work of purifying the soul and gives it strength to face the suffering and difficulties of the last hour.

The Sacrament of the Sick was instituted by Christ to give the sick spiritual aid and strength and to perfect spiritual health, including, if need be, the remission of sins. It may also restore bodily health to Christians who are seriously ill, if it helps promote their eternal salvation.

The sacrament is administered by anointing the forehead and hands, while pronouncing the words, "Through this holy anointing may the Lord in his love and mercy help you with the grace of the Holy Spirit. May the Lord who frees you from sin save you and raise you up." In the Extraordinary Form of the Roman Rite, the priest anoints the eyes, ears, nose, mouth, hands and feet, and repeats the formula each time identifying the part of the body.

There are some hints of the sacrament in the New Testament. Jesus told his disciples to "heal the sick" (Matt. 10:8). St. Mark says in 6:12–13, "and they cast out many demons, and anointed with oil many that were sick and healed them." So Jesus communicated his divine power to his disciples. The main passage proving that Anointing is a sacrament is found in the Letter of James 5:14–15, "Is anyone among you sick? Let him bring in the presbyters of the Church and let them pray over him, anointing him with oil in the name of the Lord. And the prayer of faith will save the sick man and the Lord will raise him up and if he be in sins, they shall be forgiven him."

The best way to receive this sacrament is when one is conscious and can actively participate in it. In that situation, the person should make a good confession first, then be anointed, and then receive Holy Communion as what is known as "Viaticum," that is, Communion received at the moment of "passing over" from this world of time to the Father in eternity. This is a powerful Sacrament that confers special graces. The priest should also give to the dying person the Apostolic Blessing that has a plenary indulgence attached to it. This blessing remits all the temporal punishment due to past sins. Everyone, and everyone here listening to me, should make the intention of wanting to receive the Sacrament of

Anointing of the Sick (Extreme Unction) before he or she dies. If the person is unconscious, he can still receive the Sacrament and it will, like the Sacrament of Penance, forgive all sins, if the person is properly disposed and sorry for his sins.

Just as Confirmation strengthens and perfects the grace received in Baptism, so Extreme Unction perfects the purification of the soul already accomplished by the sacrament of Penance. The Church prays in administering the sacrament: "O our Redeemer, by the grace of the Holy Spirit, cure all the ills of this sick person, heal his wounds, pardon his sins, and drive away all his pains of soul and body. In Your mercy restore him to perfect spiritual and bodily health." St. Thomas Aquinas teaches that Extreme Unction is the last Sacrament and, in a certain way, the "consummation" of all the work of purifying the soul; it prepares man for participation in glory. Because this sacrament affects the eternal destiny of the one who receives it, we should make every effort to see that our loved ones have a priest to comfort them with the sacrament when they are close to death.

We die only once, so we should prepare for it in the best way we can. Jesus has given us the Sacrament of Anointing to assist us with his grace and the Holy Spirit at the time of death. The Sacrament confers the grace we need to strengthen us, to give us peace and courage to overcome the difficulties that accompany serious illness or the frailty of old age. The Sacrament helps us to identify with the passion of Christ who died for us and through his suffering merited for us the grace of eternal life. So the Anointing of the Sick is the final preparation for the journey into eternity where we will meet our Divine Judge who will decide our status for all eternity. In order to meet him clothed in the white garment of salvation, we have to be in the state of sanctifying grace. Fortified with the final Anointing of the Sick and all the graces it confers, we have confidence, hope and peace of mind that we have saved our soul and are destined for a happy and beautiful life with God that will never end.

SACRAMENT 6: HOLY ORDERS

After having considered the sacraments of initiation and healing, we will now reflect on the Sacrament of Holy Orders which provides the Church with sacred ministers who, operating with the authority of Christ, teach, sanctify and pastor the Church of Christ by preaching the Gospel and administering the sacraments. Thus, they are instruments of Christ for the salvation and sanctification of all mankind.

One might ask, "Why is the sacrament that constitutes bishops, priests and deacons called 'Orders'?" We have to go back to ancient Rome for the answer. For the Romans, the word "order" (*ordo* in Latin) designated an established civil governing body. "Ordination" means incorporation into an *ordo*. In the Church there are established bodies which Tradition has referred to as orders or, in Latin, *ordines*. So we have the "order" of bishop, priest and deacon.

We should recall that Jesus Christ founded a hierarchical society. The Church, therefore, is not a democracy or a republic. Through Baptism we are all children of God and heirs of heaven. But a well-ordered community of millions of members requires different functions of leadership, teaching and sanctifying. In order to achieve a proper relationship between all the parts or members there must be some *order*. By the institution of Christ himself, the members of the Christian community who provide this *order* are those who have received special powers from the apostles through the imposition of hands, that is, bishops, priests and deacons. So the sacramental rite that imparts that special power in the community is called "Holy Orders."

Holy Orders is the Sacrament in which a spiritual power is conferred on one of the faithful by the imposition of hands and the prayer of the bishop, together with the grace necessary to exercise this power in a manner pleasing to God. Christ our Lord instituted Holy Orders and the priesthood on Holy Thursday at the Last

Supper when he said to his Apostles after he changed bread and wine into his Body and Blood, "Do this in memory of me" (Luke 22:19–20). And on Easter Sunday evening in the Upper Room, breathing on them—a sign of imparting the Holy Spirit—he said: "Receive the Holy Spirit. For those whose sins you forgive, they are forgiven; for those who sins you retain, they are retained" (John 20:22–23). The priest is sent by Jesus and authorized to continue in history his triple role to teach, to sanctify and to rule or pastor the people of God. He does this primarily by preaching the Gospel and by administering the Sacraments.

A bishop has the fullness of power from Jesus to perform these three functions. He also has the power of ordination, which the simple priest does not have. Bishops are descendants of the Twelve Apostles, while priests are co-workers with the bishop to help him fulfill his duty. Deacons do not have the power of the priesthood, but they do have the power of ministry; their task is to assist priests in teaching, administering the sacraments and caring for those in need. According to the institution of Jesus Christ, Holy Orders can be conferred only on men. In recent years, with the growth of feminism, the Church has made it crystal clear that she is not empowered to ordain women to the priesthood. The Catholic Church has never ordained women, but in the 2nd and 3rd centuries some of the heretical groups did do that. Since Protestants do not have the sacrament of Holy Orders, they now regularly appoint women as ministers or pastors and some even as bishops. That is one more obstacle to reunion with Rome.

By ordination one is enabled to act with divine power as a representative of Christ, as his ambassador and instrument, in his triple office of priest, prophet and king. The sacrament of Holy Orders, like Baptism and Confirmation, confers an *indelible spiritual character*, which can never be lost. So this sacrament cannot be repeated or conferred for a limited time only. Therefore, the Church prays, "Thou art a priest forever according to the order of Melchizedek."

The ordained priest receives a special grace of the Holy Spirit that makes him like Christ as priest, teacher and pastor. The priest is "another Christ" and is directed by the Church to try to imitate Christ as closely as he can. So priests are supposed to be spiritual men, close to God, who can lead others to God. As a general principle, the more holy a priest is, the more influence for good will he have over those he comes in contact with. No one can give what he does not have. If the priest does not have Christ in his heart, he cannot give him to others.

In order to become a holy priest, the Church requires priests to pray and to study: they are supposed to get a thorough grounding in theology in the seminary; after ordination they are required to pray *The Liturgy of the Hours* (formerly called *The Divine* Office or *The Breviary*) every day of their life; they are urged to pray the Rosary daily, to spend time in meditation, to study Scripture and to make an annual retreat. Bishops, as loving fathers, are supposed to see to it that priests do these things and grow spiritually, because holy priests produce holy Catholics and holy parishes.

In the past century the Church was blessed with many holy priests. Here I will mention only a few, such as, St. Pius X, Pope Pius XII, Blessed John XXIII, St. Padre Pio, St. Maximilian Kolbe, Archbishop Fulton J. Sheen, Fr. Solanus Casey, O.F.M., Fr. John Hardon, S.J., and many others. Along this line, St. Gregory Nazianzus said about priests: "We must begin by purifying ourselves before purifying others; we must be instructed to be able to instruct, become light to illuminate, draw close to God to bring him close to others, be sanctified to sanctify…" (CCC 1589). And the Holy Curé of Ars said: "The priest continues the work of redemption on earth…. If we really understood the priest on earth, we would die not of fright but of love…. The priesthood is the love of the heart of Jesus." (CCC 1551)

In the Latin Church Holy Orders is normally conferred only on candidates who have received the gift of celibacy. As you know, the rule in the Eastern Church is different, but even there only celibate priests can be consecrated as bishops.

The Catholic priesthood, given to the Church by the Lord Jesus at the Last Supper, is a great gift. In the priesthood Jesus communicates some of his divine power to weak, sinful human beings. He could have given mankind his salvific grace in other ways, but in his wisdom he has decreed to channel or funnel his grace to us through other human beings who are consecrated and anointed to be his instruments and his ambassadors.

Priests, acting in the person of Christ, have the power to offer the Holy Sacrifice of the Mass which makes the grace of Calvary present now, two thousand years after it happened. They have the power to forgive sins when, in the name of Christ, they say over a penitent sinner, "I absolve you from your sins, in the name of the Father, and of the Son and of the Holy Spirit." We all need the ministry of priests and the Church needs more priests to teach and sanctify. We all should do what we can to promote vocations to the priesthood, by prayer and by encouragement when the occasion offers itself.

SACRAMENT 7: MATRIMONY

We are all members of a family. Spouses, parents, children, siblings and relatives are the most important people in the world for us. The family is brought into existence by the marriage of a man and a woman who are old enough and eligible to enter into the state of matrimony. This morning I propose to explain the fundamentals of the Catholic doctrine on Christian marriage.

It is obvious to everyone who gives the matter some thought that marriage is a contract or agreement between a man and a woman to live together, to eat and sleep together, to love and care for one another, and to bring children into this world. The Catholic Church, unlike the Protestant groups, maintains that matrimony is a sacrament that was instituted by Jesus Christ; therefore she holds that it is a *sacred contract* because it communicates divine grace which is the supernatural life of the soul.

Because matrimony is a sacrament, the Church has certain rules or requirements that govern it. Because matrimony is a "sacred contract," God is involved in it—it is not just a secular contract that can be entered or broken according to the whim of individuals. Many years ago Archbishop Fulton J. Sheen wrote a lengthy pamphlet about this with the title "Three to Get Married." His point was, obviously, that God is involved in every Christian marriage.

Let me begin by offering you a definition of Christian marriage. It is that sacrament in which a baptized man and a baptized woman enter into a permanent communion of life and love, by mutual agreement, for the generation and education of children, and in which they receive God's grace to help them fulfill the duties of their state, to grow in holiness and to work out their eternal salvation.

A happy marriage is not the end or purpose of human existence; it is a means to the end—it is a means to grow in the love of God and to get to heaven. In a short sermon like this I cannot possibly explain everything concerning marriage. I will try to present the basics—the heart and soul of the matter.

Because human beings come in two unique forms, male and female, they are ordered to each other and they complement each other. Their union in a marital embrace often results in the conception of new human beings and the continuation of the human race. The relationship works quite well since there are about 6 billion of us on this planet at the present time. So marriage is a natural society. It was not instituted by man, but by God, who created man male and female. Since angels do not have a body, they do not come in male and female forms; this means that God created each one of them individually—angels do not have a mother and a father or brothers and sisters.

Soundly based on the Bible, the teaching of the Fathers and on Tradition, the Church teaches that marriage between two baptized Christians is more than a purely natural contract. As a result of the positive will of Christ, it is now something holy and supernatural—it is one of the seven sacraments of the Church. Since marriage is a Sacrament, this means that it confers sanctifying grace to those validly married. It means that when a Christian man and woman exchange their marriage vows they are God's instruments in the sanctification of each other. They receive the help of God's grace not only on their wedding day, but every day of their married life.

St. Paul said in Ephesians 5 which is read at many nuptial Masses: "Husbands, love your wives, just as Christ also loved the Church, and delivered himself up for her" (v. 25); and immediately he adds: "This is a great mystery—I mean in reference to Christ and to the Church" (v. 32).

What is the purpose of matrimony? The word itself gives us a hint, since it comes from the Latin word for "mother." So it is the state in which a woman becomes a mother by giving birth to children. Traditionally the Church has listed two main purposes of marriage: the generation and education of children, and the mutual assistance of the spouses who live together in a communion of life and love. Popes before Vatican II spoke of them as the primary and secondary purposes of marriage. Vatican II did not use that language, but it did list both of them as the two purposes of marriage.

Vatican II said that both purposes are essential to marriage and omitted (but did not reject) the customary distinction between the primary and secondary ends of marriage. Emphasis is given to marriage as a community of love, but the essential role of children is brought out forcefully. Thus the Fathers say in #50 of *Gaudium et Spes*: "Marriage and conjugal love are by their nature ordained toward the begetting and educating of children. Children are really the supreme gift of marriage and contribute very substantially to the welfare of their parents."

In her teaching about marriage the Church stresses two essential qualities or characteristics—its UNITY and INDISSOLUBILITY. Unity here refers to one husband with one wife, so the Church rejects polygamy and polyandry. Both are directly opposed to the teaching of the New Testament and to the two purposes of marriage. Indissolubility concerns the permanence of marriage until the death of one of the parties. In answer to a question about the legitimacy of divorce, Jesus said: "Have you not read that the creator from the beginning 'made them male and female' and that he said: 'This is why a man must leave his father and mother, and cling to his wife, and the two become one body'? They are no longer two, therefore, but one body" (Matt. 19:3–6). Jesus also said that divorcing one's wife and marrying another is adultery (Matt. 19:9).

Divorce is opposed to both ends of marriage. For unbreakable marriage is the best guarantee of the intellectual and moral education of the children; it protects the marital fidelity of husband and wife; it contributes immensely to the welfare of the family and society. And St. Paul says in Ephesians 5 that marriage is a reflection or image of the indissoluble, eternal union of Christ with his Church which he calls "a great mystery."

The annulment of some marriages, which has become more common since Vatican II, is not really a "divorce," that is a *breaking* of the marriage bond; rather, it is a declaration from the bishop that a true marriage bond never existed. Therefore, the parties are declared to be free to separate and to enter into a sacramental union with someone else, if they are fully capable of doing so.

When a Christian man and woman have freely contracted a valid marriage, and the marriage has been consummated, a sacred marriage bond is created between them which by its very nature is perpetual and exclusive. This bond is established by God himself so the Church does not have the power to break it or erase it. (See CCC 1638; CIC 1134)

It is comforting and reassuring to know that Christ raised the natural contract of marriage to the dignity of a Sacrament that confers divine grace and helps the spouses to work out their eternal salvation together. That is one reason why Archbishop Sheen spoke about "three to get married."

Because of our weakness and faults, it is not easy for any two people to live together peacefully and lovingly. Success in this risky adventure requires lots of prayer, self-discipline, selflessness and generosity. Jesus blessed marriage at the wedding feast of Cana when he changed 150 gallons of water into fine wine. The best model we have of happy family living is that of the Holy Family in Nazareth—Jesus, Mary and Joseph. They were happy and holy because they were models of virtue. The Church urges us to try to imitate them to the best of our ability.

COMMANDMENT 1: ONE GOD

I am the Lord your God. You shall have no other gods before me.

(Exod. 20:2–3: Deut. 4:6–7)

When the existence of the true God is denied or doubted, men tend to create their own gods, more to their liking. A convenient aspect of created gods is that they are much more manageable than the living God who created the heavens and the earth. We live in a time of widespread denial of God, for atheism, often disguised as a compassionate humanism, has become the "religion" of millions.

To be a real atheist, it is not necessary to tell everyone, "I am an atheist," and then proceed to offer some pseudo-argument from science or from the problem of evil in order to "prove" that God does not exist. Certainly, there are many among us who proceed in this fashion. Much more common, however, is the practice of atheism, that is, one lives <u>as if</u> there were no God, <u>as if</u> the soul were not immortal, <u>as if</u> there will be no final accountability to the Eternal Judge, <u>as if</u> there were no heaven or hell. Such foolish persons are actual or practical atheists, even though they may say that they believe in God. A notable characteristic of our time is the tremendous growth in the number of such practical atheists. Since man is born with an irresistible impulse to worship and seek God, if he denies God then he always sets up false gods and false idols, since man must worship something above himself.

The First Commandment of God gives the atheist something to think and worry about. In the first place God says, "I am the Lord your God. You shall have no other gods before me." According to the traditional understanding of the Church, this Commandment positively prescribes the practice of the virtue of religion and negatively forbids everything that is contrary to religion.

Religion is concerned with man's relationship to his Creator and Lord. The virtue of religion is the moral virtue by which we are disposed to render to God the worship he deserves. It will be very helpful for us to consider some of the implications of the worship that we owe to God. "Worship" is the name that we give to the reverence we show almighty God. Worship of God is put into practice by adoration, prayer and sacrifice.

Adoration usually suggests an image of someone bowing or kneeling or prostrate before God. Pope John Paul II sometimes prayed prostrate on the floor before the Blessed Sacrament. These bodily postures were borrowed by Christians from the external honor that was shown to oriental kings and emperors in the past. When applied to God, they signify man's total dependence on God for everything that he is and has. Since God is the source of all reality, by adoring him we give expression to that knowledge and belief. True adoration for man involves both his body and his mind, that is, an exterior sign of reverence accompanied by a mental act of submission to God.

Only God may be adored, since he alone is the Supreme Being, source of all that is. Adoration is different from the veneration offered to Mary and to the saints. Often Protestants and other non-Catholics, seeing Catholics praying the rosary or kneeling in prayer before a statue of a saint such as St. Francis or St. Theresa, accuse Catholics of offering adoration to the saints. Those who know their catechism know that this is a false accusation, because we are asking the saint in heaven to intercede for us and the statue helps us to concentrate our thoughts on what we are doing. Adoration of a lifeless stone statue would be the abomination of idolatry, which is explicitly condemned by the First Commandment.

"I am the Lord your God. You shall have no other gods before me." The First Commandment positively prescribes the worship of God and negatively forbids idolatry, superstition, sacrilege and anything that would dishonor our Creator and Lord. We might be tempted to think that the ancient peoples were crude in their worship of idols, and that therefore we do not have to worry about violations of the First Commandment because, since we have now "come of age," we are above such childish behavior.

Actually, we are creating small and large idols all the time. In a certain sense, every time we sin, every time we prefer a creature to the Creator, we are setting up "other gods" and falling away from the true God.

We all know that adoration of God is one of the basics of our Catholic religion. Adoration always involves some kind of recognition of the absolute supremacy of God and of our total dependence on him. One of the most fundamental types of adoration is "sacrifice"—an idea that is often misunderstood and in any event is not popular in today's pleasure-seeking world.

Often when we pray to God we proclaim our love and devotion to him. But St. Ignatius Loyola said in his <u>Spiritual Exercises</u> that love is shown in deeds more than in words. The requirements of a valid sacrifice are that some object, normally a desirable or valuable object, is offered to God as a sign of man's total dependence on him and of his subjection to the Lord. There is such a thing as a sacrificial mentality—readiness to give up something for the love of God. But a real sacrifice requires more than that, in order to make it clear that the offerer is sincere. It requires that the object is actually surrendered to God, destroyed, or completely removed from the possession or control of the one making the sacrifice.

In this sense, the supreme sacrifice for a human being is to offer up his life for another. And that is exactly what Jesus himself did for us on Calvary—he offered up his life to his Father as a propitiation for our sins. He took our sins upon himself and suffered in our place, he, the perfectly innocent One.

The Mass is a re-presentation now, in an unbloody manner, of the bloody sacrifice of the Cross two thousand years ago. Since it is a re-offering of Jesus on Calvary, the Mass is rightly referred to as "the holy *Sacrifice* of the Mass," although we do not hear this expression much today. It has been replaced by the more general and vague "liturgy," which also applies to the celebration of the other sacraments.

Every dimension of human existence can, and often does, require sacrifices. There are certain things that we have to give up, that are taken away from us, and so forth. But a sacrifice to God, a religious sacrifice, is one that is *freely given* to God as a sign of reverence and submission to him. Such sacrifices are very meritorious in the sight of God, because they are basically acts of love of God and that is what God wants from us more than anything else—love. Love must be free; it cannot be forced and it cannot be bought.

In addition to adoration and sacrifice, the worship of God mandated by the First commandment is also carried out by personal prayer. In the Bible there are hundreds of references to prayer. Abraham prayed, Moses prayed, David prayed. The incomparable Psalms of the Old Testament are one hundred and fifty prayers of great variety and incredible beauty.

When we read the Gospels we see that Jesus prayed often—frequently spending the whole night in prayer. He prayed for forty days in the desert in preparation for his public ministry. It was during this time that the devil tempted him to abandon his mission of saving the human race. By prayer and fasting Jesus overcame the devil.

Jesus set a good example, but he also urged his disciples to pray. "Watch and pray, that you may not enter into temptation. The spirit indeed is willing, but the flesh is weak" (Matt. 26:41). St. Paul wrote to his converts: "Pray without ceasing. In all things give thanks; for this is the will of God in Christ Jesus regarding you all" (1 Thess. 5:16–18). And St. James said: "The unceasing prayer of a just man is of great avail" (5:16).

So the lesson from Holy Scripture is clear: we should be constant in prayer. That, of course, is easier said than done. Many people find prayer difficult, either because they think they do not know how to pray or because they are so distracted by their interests and anxieties that they cannot concentrate on what they are doing.

Actually, prayer is quite simple. It is similar to our dealing with our loved ones. When we are with them we are aware of their presence, we talk to them, we ask them for favors. Our heavenly Father is always with us. He is aware of our distress; he knows what we need even before we ask him for anything. He will grant our requests if we ask him, but he does want us to ask.

Idolatry in the strict sense means the worship of some image or "idol." Such idols are usually artistic representations of creatures which are believed to have super-human powers. The idols can be representations of outstanding men, such as the Caesars of the Roman Empire, or images of various animals, birds, reptiles. Before the advent of Christ, such idol worship was common in the ancient world. Christianity was quite successful in rooting out idolatry, so much so that it has been of rare occurrence in the Western world for many centuries.

The purpose of idolatry is to show divine honors to a creature which is thought to be a supreme being of some kind. As such it is an act of religion—though false religion. Idolatry can proceed from ignorance, as when the idolaters do not know the true God and so select some powerful creature, such as the sun or the moon, as the object of their reverence. As in all worship, the purpose is to appease the god, to ward off dangers and to ask for blessings of various kinds. Idolatry was an abomination to the Israelites of the Old Testament. The sacred authors delighted in heaping scorn on the idols of the pagans among whom they lived. Thus we read in Psalms 115: "their idols, in silver and gold, products of human skill, have mouths, but never speak, eyes, but never see, ears, but never hear... and not a sound from their throats."

Since idolatry involves a denial of the sovereignty of God over his creation, it is a direct violation of the First Commandment and is an offense against the virtue of religion. It is also opposed to the theological virtues of charity and faith, because it does not render to God the adoration which is his due and it involves a denial of the truth that faith professes.

The number of possible objects for adoration, in place of the true God who is, is not many. Some choose to worship themselves or some other individual. Thus, we now often hear such expressions as "I adore you." In the realm of creatures there are a few that give the appearance of being infinite, so they are better suited to be made into idols for worship. The most common are: money, political or economic power, fame or glory, scholarship and the renown that goes with it, sexual pleasure and, on the lowest scale, food and drink. If a person's whole life is dedicated to the pursuit of one of these, or a combination of them, to the total neglect of God almighty, then that person is guilty of idolatry. He or she is giving divine honors to a creature, instead of worshiping the Creator of all things. The First Commandment warns us to reject all such false idols.

When we take part in the liturgy of the Church, which is worship of the only true God, we are obeying and fulfilling the First Commandment: "I am the Lord your God. You shall have no other gods before me."

COMMANDMENT 2: GOD'S NAME

You shall not take the name of the Lord your God in vain.

(Exod. 20:7; Deut. 4:11)

Today we will reflect on the Second Commandment which forbids taking the name of God in vain. The Bible threatens punishment on those who misuse the sacred name of the Lord. Thus we read in Exodus 20:7, "You shall not take the name of the Lord your God in vain; for the Lord will not hold him guiltless who takes his name in vain."

With Shakespeare we might ask, "What is in a name?" The Israelites of the Old Testament did not make a clear distinction, as we do, between the name of God and God himself. Therefore the name was to be treated with the same respect that one would show to God himself.

By the Second Commandment we are directed always to speak with reverence of God, of Mary, of the saints and of holy things. When the holy name of God is invoked, it should be either in prayer or in an attitude of reverence for our Lord and Creator. Our lips and tongue betray what we are. If we have interior reverence and respect for God and all things holy, then we will be most careful in speaking about them. On the other hand, if we habitually disregard God's law, if we rarely think of God or if we resent God's creative authority over us, then this will manifest itself by means of the words that cross our lips. Thus, it is truly distressing to God-fearing Catholics to have to associate with persons who constantly take the name of the Lord in vain in order to give emphasis to a statement.

Parents should set a good example for their children by avoiding such profanity; they should also not tolerate the misuse of God's holy name by their children. When I was a boy children would get their mouth washed out with soap as a punishment for taking God's name in vain. Such a remedy may not be a certain cure, but it surely got the point across.

What is in a name? For one thing, eternal salvation. The Old Testament tells us repeatedly that the holy name of God is to be praised, that the Lord will save those who call upon him for assistance. There is great power in the name of Jesus Christ, since Jesus means "savior," and Christ means "Messiah" or "the anointed one of the Lord." Stressing the power inherent in the name of Jesus, St. Peter told the Jewish leaders in Jerusalem, according to St. Luke's account in Acts 4:12, "There is salvation in no one else, for there is no other name under heaven given among men by which we must be saved."

Perhaps the Second Commandment is one that we do not often advert to. But the sincere Christian is one who has great reverence for God and for his holy name. In this age of increasing vulgarity, profanity, atheism and ridicule of God and his saints, we Catholics should be especially careful, not only from a desire of worship of God but also in order to make reparation to him, always to use God's holy name with great reverence. Let ours be the sentiment of the psalmist in Psalm 112:2–3, "Blessed be the name of the Lord both now and forever. From the rising to the setting of the sun is the name of the Lord to be praised."

God's name may be abused by taking an oath unnecessarily which means calling on God as a witness to the truth of an assertion or to the sincerity of a promise. In a court of law one can take an oath, but it must be done reverently. Jesus himself took an oath before the Jewish Council. But his will is that we should normally deal with each other without having to confirm what we say by oaths. Jesus said: "I say to you not to swear at all... let your speech by 'Yes, yes'; 'No, no'; and whatever is beyond these comes from the evil one" (see Matt. 5:34–37).

However, at times and for very serious reasons, it is necessary to give special force to what a person says by calling upon God to witness to the truth of a statement. Thus, law courts often require witnesses to take an oath to support the truth of their assertions. Deliberately to tell a lie while under such an oath is the sin of perjury. Perjury is a mortal sin, since it blasphemes God who knows all things and is infinite truth. It is also a sin to swear an oath without sufficient reason or without being absolutely sure of the truth to which one swears.

Two serious sins against the Second Commandment are blasphemy and cursing. Blasphemy is any speech or gesture that manifests contempt for God. The blasphemer is one who, while believing in God and recognizing his holiness, deliberately insults him out of fear, anger, hatred, despair or some other deep human emotion. Blasphemy is a mortal sin by its very nature because it is directed against the infinite majesty of God. There may be mitigating circumstances, such as uncontrollable rage, that would make the sin venial by reason of lack of due deliberation, but the sin of blasphemy of itself is a serious offense against God.

It is blasphemous, for example, to call God stupid, cruel or unjust, or to shake one's fist against heaven. Blasphemy was considered such a serious offence in the OT that it was punished by stoning to death. It was the chief accusation made against Jesus by the leaders of Israel because he said he was the Son of God (see Matt. 26:63–66).

Cursing is also a violation of the Second Commandment. To curse is to call down evil on someone or something. Although in the OT we see a number of examples of the cursing of enemies, in the NT the cursing of enemies is strictly forbidden. Jesus commanded his followers to love their enemies, to pray for them and to be reconciled with them, if possible. He taught us in the Our Father to pray: "Forgive us our trespasses as we forgive those who trespass against us." This puts us in a very dangerous situation. For, if the forgiveness we receive from the Father is conditioned by the forgiveness we show to others, then, if we wish to have our sins forgiven, we ought to show mercy and kindness to those who have offended us.

Catholic moralists distinguish between cursing things less than man and cursing persons. To curse things and animals is wrong mainly because of the impatience involved. The overused expression "God damn" this or that has lost much of its original meaning, but its use is an offense against the Second Commandment and it should be sedulously avoided. To curse people by wishing them evil is wrong—especially if moral evil and eternal damnation are called down on them. Such an act is always seriously sinful if done with full deliberation.

Language, speech, articulated thought are magnificent gifts of God. This point is made brilliantly by professor Higgins in the play and film *My Fair Lady*. Without speech man would be reduced to the level of the brute beasts; with it he can aspire to the company of the angels and of the Lord God himself. Let us strive, with God's grace, to avoid all blasphemies and curses and to use our tongues to praise and to bless. God bless you.

COMMANDMENT 3: SUNDAY

Remember to keep holy the Sabbath day

(Exodus 20:8; Deut. 4:12)

Because the universe, the earth and mankind belong to God who created them, we must spend some time on a regular basis in worshipping him and giving him thanks. Nature itself seems to require this, as we see plainly manifested in the religious customs of most peoples and cultures.

God revealed his precise will in this matter to the Israelites in the Old Testament when he gave Moses his Third Commandment: "Remember to keep holy the Sabbath day" (Exod. 20:8). To the early Israelites this means that no work was to be done on the Sabbath or Saturday. By the time of Jesus there were synagogues in the towns, so the people would gather there for prayer and instruction on the holy day, as they still do.

The early Christians changed the day of worship from Saturday, the last day of the week, to Sunday, the first day. The principal reasons given in the tradition of the Church for this change are that Jesus rose from the dead on Sunday and also sent down the Holy Spirit on his Church on this day. Another reason given by St. Justin Martyr is that God created the world on this day, the first day of the week. Sunday also reminds us of Baptism and the new creation which began with our Lord's Resurrection. Sunday was also called "the Lord's Day" (Latin: *dies dominica;* see Rev. 1:10).

Please note these beautiful words of St. Maxim on Turin: "We hold the Lord's Day in reverence and celebrate it solemnly, because on that day our Savior, like the rising sun, shone in the light of his glorious resurrection after conquering the darkness of hell; this day is called Sunday, because Christ, the Sun of Justice, fills it with light."

In the first centuries of the Church there were no laws enjoining attendance at Mass on Sundays under pain of sin. It was simply assumed that all Christians would be present at the Eucharistic liturgy, if at all possible.

As the centuries passed by, however, the faith of many grew cool and they did not attend Mass. Thus, from the sixth to the thirteenth centuries Church laws requiring attendance became more explicit, culminating in legislation for the whole Church that Mass attendance is obligatory every Sunday and holy day for all Catholics who have reached their seventh birthday. So every Sunday is a holy day of obligation.

There are six precepts of the Church explained in the Catechism. The very first precept of the Church is: to assist at Mass on all Sundays and holy days of obligation, like Christmas and the Ascension.

Since Vatican II there has been a great reluctance on the part of bishops, priests, theologians and religion teachers to talk about the duties or responsibilities of the faithful in terms of "obligations," "commandments," and "binding under the pain of sin." These expressions are not used much in our day, but the reality they signify has not changed.

Thus all Catholics over seven years of age who have sufficient use of reason are bound under pain of mortal sin to attend Mass on Sunday, unless they are excused for a good reason. Naturally, sickness, the need to care for a sick child, great distance and similar circumstances excuse one from this obligation.

All Catholics, therefore, have a serious obligation in conscience to attend Mass on Sundays and holy days. Holy Communion is not required, but attendance at Mass is. Clergy and religious teachers of all kinds have the corresponding duty to communicate this truth to the faithful. The basic reason for this is simple: in order to lead a good Christian life it is necessary to worship God regularly, and often to receive Holy Communion. In this way we are strengthened to overcome the temptations from the world, the flesh and the devil and to strive for holiness.

Faithful observance of the Third Commandment requires two things, namely, assistance at Mass and abstinence from unnecessary work. When God on Mount Sinai commanded that every seventh day should be kept holy, he said to Moses: "Six days you shall labor, and do all your work; but the seventh day is a Sabbath to the Lord your God; in it you shall not do any work, you, or your son, or your daughter..." (Exod. 20:9–10).

In 321 A.D. the Roman Emperor Constantine ordered that Sunday was to be observed by all as a day of worship and rest. Most legal codes of Christian nations since that time have included some laws concerning the Sunday rest. The thirteen colonies had such laws as do most, perhaps all, of the fifty states at the present time.

The Sunday rest is something that characterizes Christian civilization, and is usually not found among non-Christians, such as in China and India. One may observe with considerable accuracy that the level of observance of Sunday—both with regard to worship and with regard to rest—is a fair measure of the intensity of Christian faith in any country. With each passing year, however, we are witnessing the rapid dechristianization or secularization of American culture. Is it not true that at the same time we are seeing more and more gross violations of the Sunday rest, more stores advertising that they are open 24/7? Catholics can show their disapproval of this by avoiding all unnecessary shopping on Sunday, by staying away from the local mall.

By not working one day a week, on the Lord's Day, the Christian bears witness to the fact that he truly believes in the promises of Jesus Christ. He shows that his ultimate trust is in God and not in material goods. He is saying in effect: I pass up the opportunity to earn more money on the Lord's Day because I know that I am made for heaven; my nature and my eternal destiny infinitely surpass the things of this world. The pagans work on Sunday because they have no hope in eternal life—and perhaps because they do not know any better.

What does the Sunday rest mean for an American in the 21st century? That is a difficult question to answer. The main purpose, of course, is so that we will have the time and opportunity to attend Mass, to hear the Word of God and to receive our Lord in the Blessed Sacrament. Some activities that are in conformity with the Sunday observance are: reading the Bible or the life of some saint; praying the Rosary; engaging in conversation about God and the things of the spirit.

Sunday should also be a day of joy and relaxation. It is the time for a family meal, for healthy recreation, for sport, for reading or study, for taking a stroll or for going for a Sunday drive. In these and similar activities we can both praise God for his goodness and refresh our body and mind after the week's work.

Since the time of Moses, abstinence from all unnecessary work has been an essential part of the Sunday observance. Perhaps you have heard that the Church forbids all "servile" work on Sunday. Formerly "servile work" was defined as hard physical labor; thus, digging ditches, plowing, splitting wood, and so forth were said to be "servile" and so were forbidden on Sunday except in cases of emergency or real necessity.

In modern times so many exceptions have been placed on the meaning of servile work by moral theologians that it is just about impossible to lay down general rules. Thus, many men and women who spend the whole week behind a desk find real refreshment in working in their garden, mowing the lawn, or doing other chores around the house. Although these activities require physical labor, they are not now considered to be "servile" in the situation of contemporary technological America. Two hours of such work on Sunday is not a violation of the Sunday rest.

It seems to me that what all should try to do is to observe the spirit of Sunday—worship and rest and joy. If some kind of work does not fit into that pattern, and is truly unnecessary and burdensome, then it should be avoided. If anyone has a serious doubt about whether or not he or she is violating the Sunday rest, then that person should seek the advice of a priest.

COMMANDMENT 4:
HONOR PARENTS

Honor your father and your mother, that your days may
be long in the land which the Lord your God gives you.
(Exodus 20:12)

Each of the Ten Commandments covers a special area of human concern. Each Commandment also presents certain difficulties of observance. Today perhaps more than ever before, because of the anti-authority current in modern society, the Fourth Commandment takes on vital importance. The Commandment itself, as proclaimed by Moses, says: "Honor your father and your mother, that your days may be long in the land which the Lord your God gives you" (Exod. 20:12).

God therefore commands that we "honor" our natural parents. The divine command merely reaffirms what the natural law requires, since it is obvious that none of us would ever reach maturity if it were not for our parents, or someone else who takes their place, who brought us into the world and cared for us until we were old enough to provide for ourselves.

Man by his very nature is a social being. This means that he cannot either come into existence or develop into a mature person without the help and cooperation of other human beings. Associations of human beings are called "communities." By his birth the child is inserted into a number of different communities, the principal ones being the family, the state and the church. Communities can function only if there is some authority that directs the members, in one way or another, to the stated or accepted goals of the community. Authority is here taken to mean the moral power or right to direct others to some end.

Since the family is a community it follows that it possesses some authority. And since the family comes from God, the authority that resides in it also comes from God. That authority is located in the father and the mother. So God tells us through Moses to honor our father and mother. The "honor" due to parents has been understood in the Church for centuries to mean that we should love, reverence and obey our parents.

We love our parents by wishing them well, spending some time with them, praying for them and helping them in any way we can. We reverence our parents by speaking and acting towards them in a kindly manner, by seeking their advice as occasion warrants, by readily accepting their corrections and by patiently putting up with their faults.

Children should obey the lawful commands of their parents as long as they live under parental authority. In fact, children can sin grievously by disobeying the strict command of a parent in an important matter. However, children who do not live any longer under parental authority are not bound to follow the directions of their parents, though one should at least listen to what they have to say. But even adult children are subject to parental authority in certain areas of everyday living, such as times for meals, coming home at night, etc., as long as they live under their parents' roof.

Many parents have a difficult time of it today in getting their children to obey them. There are many reasons for this. We live in an age that glorifies personal freedom, sometimes to the point of license, at the expense of authority. Children are frequently urged—by the media, by their peers, and sometimes even by their teachers in school—to challenge and resist parental authority. This gives rise to serious conflicts in many families. It seems to me that early and frequent schooling of children in the divine command of obedience to one's parents would help to improve this situation. Also, parents must insist on and require reasonable obedience from their children from the earliest age.

A very serious problem now related to the Fourth Commandment is the care of mother and father in their old age. Some "rest homes" are good, but many are a scandal. No general rule can be laid down in this matter, but children who place their parents in one of these homes should see to it that they are not using the home as a way of avoiding their duties to their parents. The obligation to obey parents ceases at some point, but the obligation to love and reverence them never ceases. If a parent is placed in such a home it must be done for the right reason and after all other possibilities have been explored.

Under the Fourth Commandment are included our relations to the members of our family and also our relations to other authorities, such as employers, teachers, the state and the Church. Let us reflect on the implications of some of these relationships.

By the Fourth Commandment we are commanded to love our brothers and sisters, to behave well towards them, to put up with their faults (they must also learn to put up with our faults!) and to help them when we can. Older brothers and sisters should look after the younger ones. Those individuals who are born into a large family are the beneficiaries of a special blessing from God.

Relatives too are closer to us than other people, and are therefore deserving of more attention. We should at least show our affection for them and try to help them in any way we can when they are in need. "Help" in this case does not always mean money; very often it can mean a kind word, or a visit to them when they are sick, or even a card at Christmas or on the occasion of a birthday.

By the Fourth commandment we are also directed to be obedient to all lawful authority. That is a very broad statement which requires many qualifications and which is very difficult to apply in many concrete situations. One clear case is the relation between teachers and students. Parents are the primary teachers of their children and have the primary responsibility for their upbringing. But in our society parents are not capable of properly educating their children, so they send them to school. In sending their children to a school the parents are sharing their authority over their children with the teachers and school authorities. In virtue of the Fourth Commandment, therefore, students have the obligation to respect and obey their teachers in those areas that pertain to the teacher's competence. Of course, we are assuming here that the teachers remain within the limits of their competence and do not violate the rights either of the parents or the students.

Another important area of human relations covered by the Fourth Commandment is the matter of respect for old people. The aged have a special dignity. In the course of their lives they have gathered great experience; many have worked very hard, have risked their lives for their country, have sacrificed for their children. It is absolutely shocking the way many old people are treated in the United States. Many live in terror—terror of being mugged or killed by teenage thugs. In New York City there are reports in the news often about violence inflicted on old people—usually by the young. One sociologist said recently that America is the first society in the history of the world in which the elderly live in fear of the young.

We should all reflect on both our attitude toward the elderly and our treatment of them. We read in the Bible (Lev. 19:32): "Stand up in the presence of the aged, and show respect for the old."

If it were not for our parents we would never have been born, we would not have been created by God, we would not be here today. Both the natural law and the revealed law of the Gospel tell us that we should honor our parents. We do that by showing them respect in many ways in this life, and by praying for them while they are living and especially after they have died and are in the hands of God.

"Honor your father and your mother, that your days may be long in the land which the Lord your God gives you." God bless you.

COMMANDMENT 5: HUMAN LIFE

You shall not kill.

(Exod. 20:13; Deut. 5:17)

The Fifth Commandment is, "You shall not kill" (Exod. 20:13). There are very many ramifications of God's commandment to respect life, especially today in our society when there are so many threats against human life on all sides: biological, sociological, political, environmental, economical and medical.

A Catholic accepts as a datum of faith that a personal God exists and that he created, by a free act of his will, the world and everything that is in the entire universe. God's creation is good, desirable and to be respected: "God saw all he had made, and indeed it was very good" (Gen. 1:31).

The pinnacle of God's material creation is man who in some way, because of his intellect and will, actually mirrors the Lord God himself, for "God created man in the image of himself, in the image of God he created him, male and female he created them" (Gen. 1:27).

Without going into the whole of Bible history, suffice it to say that man is much more than a material, biological being who lives out his "three score and ten" years on this earth and then returns, like the beasts of the forest, to the dust and slime from which he was taken. No. Man has an eternal destiny. He has an immortal soul that is destined for eternal happiness in a most personal, intimate union of knowledge and love with God forever.

The first and most important of all man's natural rights is his right to life, for if his life is taken away then all other rights become meaningless. All other rights of man are based on his unalienable right to life. The Lord gives and the Lord takes away. In the Christian view of the world, God is the source of all life; he is also the Master of life. He gives it and only he can justly and legitimately take it away. This means then that, according to the Christian worldview, no human person, no organization and no state agency has the right to dispose arbitrarily of human life. Often we use the word "sacred" to characterize God and those things closely associated with him. Because of man's close association with God perhaps it is best to describe his life as "sacred." When so designated it means that man is to keep his hands off human life—at least in the sense of trying to dispose of it for his own selfish purposes.

Accordingly, God forbids one man to kill another, as happened in the case of the first recorded murder when Cain slew his brother Abel (Gen. 4:8). In the tradition of the Church and in the explanations of the theologians, this Commandment has always been understood in the sense of "You shall not commit murder," murder being here understood in the sense of the unjust killing of an innocent person. Certainly the Commandment does not apply to the killing of animals as a source of food supply. It directly concerns the killing of other human beings. However, both the Bible and the tradition of the Church affirm the liceity and the morality of killing another human being in certain, well-defined circumstances, such as killing an unjust aggressor against oneself or against a third party who is innocent, or the killing that is involved in a just, defensive war. But it is always evil directly to kill an innocent person as happens in murder and abortion.

The profound difference in outlook between Catholics and all types of atheists and materialists stands out sharply in the matter of respect for human life. For the pragmatic atheist/materialist human life is basically a natural resource like fresh water or crude oil; it is to be used for the betterment of the state or human society. For them, when human life becomes "useless," in the sense that it does not contribute to the G.N.P. in some way, it is to be eliminated the same way one disposes of garbage. This mentality explains the attitude of atheistic materialists in questions of abortion, infanticide and euthanasia. Since for them man is the only absolute, it is up to man alone to decide who shall live and who shall die. In the last century there were many examples of such disregard for human life on the part of communists in Russia and China, and on the part of the Nazis in Hitler's Germany.

The Catholic view of human life is worlds apart from that of the atheistic secular humanists. For the Catholic, human life is sacred, it is inviolable, because it was given by God almighty. And not only did God bestow on us human life, but he also, by an absolutely free act of love, raised man to the supernatural level and so destined him for eternal life in the beatific, face-to-face vision of God. Because men have a supernatural destiny as the adopted children of God and heirs of heaven, they have a dignity that is innate and that surpasses any honor that can be conferred by this world. In the concrete, this means that no one may "use" human life for his own selfish purposes, whether it be for the good of the state or for the progress of science. Vatican II expressed this clearly in its decree on Religious Liberty where it states the importance of human dignity.

Since life is a gift from God, we are not absolute masters of our own life. It is more accurate to say that we are "stewards" or "caretakers" of our lives and that God will demand from us an accounting of our stewardship. We did not cause ourselves or bring ourselves into existence.

Why did God give life to man? He gave man life so that he might grow in the knowledge and love of God, practice virtue and merit eternal life with the help of God's grace. God in his providence allots a certain amount of time to each one of us in order to accomplish the purpose for which he created us. In order to "work out our salvation in fear and trembling" we need first of all to live so that we can respond to God's loving Word. This being the case, as a good steward man must take care of his life, using all the ordinary means put at his disposal by God. It is contrary to the will of God, and therefore sinful, unreasonably to injure one's body or to shorten one's life.

The anti-life crowd in America is now pushing hard for physician- assisted suicide or euthanasia. It is already available in three States—Oregon, Washington, and Montana. It is also being actively pursued in several other states. Since euthanasia is the unjust killing of an innocent person, it is murder and so is strictly forbidden by the Fifth Commandment. When we talk about euthanasia and "death with dignity" we must be careful to know precisely what is at issue. What the law of God forbids is the DIRECT killing of an innocent human being, whether healthy or unhealthy, whether a fetus or an old man. This means that no positive steps may be taken to terminate the life of another; thus, no shooting, no lethal injections, no lethal pills, and so forth. It also requires that all of the ORDINARY means of sustaining life must be used until the person dies of natural causes. But there is no moral obligation to employ EXTRAORDINARY means to prolong life—means that are especially burdensome, costly and invasive.

Our government has embraced a "culture of death." More than 50 million abortions have been performed since the Supreme Court approved abortion in 1973. Abortion is simply murder—it is the killing of an innocent person. Condemnation of abortion as murder has been the constant teaching of the Catholic Church since the first century. Popes from Pius XI to Benedict XVI have condemned it explicitly and John Paul II wrote a whole encyclical letter about it, THE GOSPEL OF LIFE.

Vatican II reiterated the constant tradition of the Church when it declared: "Life must be protected with the utmost care from the moment of conception: abortion and infanticide are abominable crimes" (GS 51). The reason why the Church is now attacked by the secularists is because of her defense of human life and her teaching about sex and marriage.

Other violations of human dignity forbidden by the Fifth Commandment are sterilization of men and women and unnecessary mutilation of the body, such as harvesting organs like heart and liver and kidneys from persons who are still alive. That is a medical or hospital form of murder of the innocent. The end does not justify the means. Because a young person needs a new heart does not justify taking a beating heart from someone else who is still alive.

We should do all we can by prayer and wise voting to protect innocent human life.

COMMANDMENT 6:
NO ADULTERY

You shall not commit adultery.

(Exod. 20:14; Deut. 5:18)

There is perhaps no area of modern life, especially in the post-Christian West, where the opposition between Catholic faith and practice on the one hand, and contemporary values and mores on the other, is more evident than it is in the whole area of sex. To put the matter very simply, for the believing Catholic sex is sacred because it was created by God for the purpose of transmitting human life; for pagans and secularized Christians, sex is for fun—it is a source of play and self-gratification for the autonomous person who uses it where, when and how he or she wishes with no reference whatsoever to a Creator-God.

For the most part, the basic position one takes on sex will be an indication of one's values and practice in such matters as adultery, fornication, masturbation, homosexuality, pornography, contraception and divorce. The believer will regulate his thinking and life in accordance with the laws of God and the teaching of the Church; the American pagan will think and live on the basis of "personal conscience," relativism and popular cultural standards as set by the media and the peer group.

God said to the Israelites of old through Moses: "You shall not commit adultery." As it was understood in the OT, adultery was primarily a violation of justice, since by adultery the rights of a third party are usurped. Jesus elevated the relationship between a man and his wife to a higher level than it was under the old law because he made marriage a sacrament. He also made it very clear that adultery, and even adulterous thoughts, are contrary to the virtue of chastity. For he says in Matt. 5:27–28: "You have heard it was said to the ancients, 'You shall not commit adultery.' But I say to you that anyone who so much as looks with lust at a woman has already committed adultery with her in his heart."

It is clear that the Sixth Commandment explicitly forbids adultery, which is an act of sexual intercourse between a married man and a woman not his wife, or between a married woman and a man not her husband. The specific characteristic of the sin of adultery is that at least one of the partners is married; if neither party engaging in sexual relations is married the sin is called "fornication."

Implicitly the Sixth Commandment also forbids all impurity and immodesty in words, looks and actions, whether alone or with others. What do we mean by impurity or unchastity? Impurity is any thought, word, look or deed with oneself or with another by which the sexual appetite is aroused outside of marriage, and even in marriage when contrary to the purpose for which God instituted the married state. Some of the chief sins against purity are adultery, fornication, deliberate actions with oneself or others performed to arouse the sexual appetite, such as masturbation or homosexuality. Deliberately looking at pornography of any kind, especially on the Internet, should be included here.

Modesty is a virtue which is very closely related to purity or chastity—its purpose is to protect chastity, as it were to build up defenses around it. Modesty is the moral virtue that moderates and controls the impulse for sexual display in men and women. Thus, looked at from the negative point of view, immodesty is any deliberate thought, word or action that tends towards impurity. Sins against modesty include such things as looks, touches, conversation, songs, reading, suggestive clothing motivated by the desire for sexual pleasure.

From the positive side, by the Sixth Commandment we are commanded to be modest and pure in our behavior. Chastity is a moral virtue which rightly regulates all voluntary expression of sexual pleasure in marriage and excludes it altogether outside the married state. Chastity also contributes very much to the preservation and strengthening of the other virtues.

When I was studying moral theology in the seminary a shrewd old professor used to tell us over and over again: "Don't worry about theft; study and master the Sixth Commandment. That's where you will encounter most of your difficulties in the confessional." There is much truth in that advice. For most people, the most common sins are those of the tongue, excess in eating and drinking and unchaste thoughts and acts.

The sexual instinct in man and woman is very strong. If it were not, very few men and women, it seems to me, would voluntarily assume the rights and obligations of the married state, thereby committing themselves to each other for life and committing themselves to raising the children that God might send them. Human beings are also very weak, because of concupiscence which is a result of Original Sin. Their weakness is especially evident in violations of the Sixth Commandment—as our old professor intimated.

Man's weakness in the face of his powerful sexual instinct has led some moral philosophers, and even some Christians to look upon sex and sexual intercourse as something evil. Such an attitude is contrary to the teaching of the Bible and the constant tradition of the Church. At the very beginning of the Bible we read: "God created man in the image of himself, in the image of God he created him, male and female he created them. God blessed them, saying to them, 'Be fruitful, multiply, fill the earth and conquer it'" (Gen. 1:27–28). Thus the sexual organs are good and the sexual act in marriage is also good, because of its two-fold God-given purpose: the generation of children and as an expression of committed love between husband and wife.

There is no escaping the fact that sex is essentially related to the transmission of human life. Since human life comes from God in a special way, it enjoys a certain inviolability—it is sacred. In the generation of children, husband and wife are cooperating with the creative power of God in a very special way. Most Catholic theologians have held that each human soul is immediately created by God at the moment of conception. Pope Pius XII, in his 1950 encyclical *Humani Generis*, taught: "The Catholic faith obliges us to hold firmly that souls are immediately created by God" (D 3027).

Because of its relationship to human life, the Church has always considered sex important. In accordance with Scripture, she has always insisted that the love and service of God cannot be reconciled with adultery, fornication, promiscuity, lustful desires, self-abuse, homosexual acts and pornography. Such acts violate the basic human good involved in the proper use of the sex faculty and so are a misuse of God's generous gifts. In a word, they are seriously sinful because they run contrary to man's true good as revealed in the Bible and also as known through the use of human reason (cf. Rom. 1).

According to the Bible and the constant teaching of the Church, sexual intercourse is a moral good only within the context of marriage. This is a hard saying and it is very difficult for many people to understand. Why, we are often asked, is pre-nuptial sex not morally permissible if the couple truly love each other? The Church replies by saying that sexual intercourse represents and expresses a permanent, mutual gift of self which is realized only in marriage. Here, obviously, we are touching on the *symbolic* nature of the sex act, since in human persons sex is not just a mechanical, strictly biological activity. For sexual intercourse between a man and a woman gives exterior expression to the interior love that exists between them. If it is not an expression of love, then it is a form of violence, such as rape or some type of prostitution.

The permanence and monogamous nature of marriage are based, in Catholic thinking, on two factors: the education of children to maturity and the growth of love and friendship between a man and his wife. It does not take very long to conceive and bear children, but it is a long process to raise them and educate them to maturity. But even after children have reached adulthood they still need and depend on their parents in many ways. Also, growth in love and mutual self-giving takes a lifetime. Accordingly, sexual activity must be confined to marriage and marriage, in Catholic teaching, is both monogamous and indissoluble. This teaching, I know, is commonly rejected today by American pagans, but that does not make it any less true.

These are some of the basic truths included in the Sixth Commandment, "You shall not commit adultery." We should all pray for light and understanding of God's law and for the grace to follow it and make it a reality in our life. Our eternal salvation depends on it. God will not be mocked, no matter what modern pagans may say. St. Paul put it well when he said: "It is a fearful thing to fall into the hands of the living God." At the same time, our God is a God who is rich in mercy and he knows better than we do how weak we are. Amen.

COMMANDMENT 7: STEALING

You shall not steal.

(Exod. 20:15; Deut. 5:19; Matt. 19:18)

One of the basic principles of the natural law is respecting the property of others. It is a matter of justice not to harm another in his person or in his property. The same truth is expressed in the Seventh Commandment of God found in the book of Exodus in the Old Testament: "You shall not steal." There is also a commandment against coveting the goods of others which we will treat in the Tenth Commandment.

There are many ramifications to the commandment about stealing; today I can deal only with some of the most important ones.

Going beyond this general law, the OT also forbids robbery, usury, fraud and the deliberate destruction of other people's property. There are special precepts that deal with false weights and measures for those selling good to others, and precepts that deal with a just wage for a day's work.

Jesus, followed by his faithful Apostles, especially Sts. Peter and Paul, repeated the Mosaic denunciation of thievery. For example, when the rich young man asked him what he should do to attain eternal life, our Savior told him to keep the Commandments, quoting, among others, the Seventh Commandment, "You must not steal" (Mark 10:19). St. Paul told those who were thieves before their conversion to change their ways: "Anyone who was a thief must stop stealing; he should try to find some useful manual work instead, and be able to do some good by helping others that are in need" (Eph. 4:28).

What do we mean by stealing? Catholic moralists define stealing as the deliberate taking of something against the reasonable will of the owner. To steal secretly is called "theft," while using or threatening violence in the act of taking is called "robbery." Thus, mugging is a type of robbery; cheating, keeping found articles whose owners could easily be discovered, neglecting to pay one's debts, are considered equivalent to theft.

Theft and robbery are contrary to the natural law and also to the revealed law of the Ten Commandments, as we have seen. The fact that God's law forbids stealing is an implicit affirmation of the right to the private ownership of property that belongs to others. For, if there were no right of ownership, then everything would belong to everybody and there would be no such thing as stealing: everyone could help himself at any time to whatever he wanted. Obviously, such a situation would result in chaos and would be the end of any kind of peaceful social life.

Robbery, which includes a threat to violence, is certainly a mortal sin. Theft can be either a venial sin or a mortal sin, depending on the amount stolen and the circumstances of the person from whom it is taken. It is often difficult to distinguish between light and grave matter, that is, what would be enough for a venial sin or a mortal sin. In the past, moralists have held that stealing a day's wages from a working man would be a mortal sin; that changes as the economy changes. In absolute numbers, stealing from a company or big corporation $500 or more would surely be a mortal sin.

Someone who has stolen money or property goes to confession and seeks absolution in the Sacrament of Penance. What is he required to do? The constant teaching of the Church on this point is that one who has stolen the property of another, such as money, a TV set, a camera, or whatever, and one who has inflicted unjust damage on the property of another, such as deliberately damaging his car, is bound to RESTITUTION before he or she can be fully forgiven. The word comes from the Latin *restituere* which means " to restore something," "to set it up where it had been." Restitution then is the repairing of an injury, the righting of a wrong.

In the eyes of God and the Church it is not sufficient for forgiveness that the thief repent of his sins; in order to demonstrate that he is truly repentant he must also give back what he has unjustly taken from a fellow human being. The obligation of restitution is based on the natural law. Since ownership is a true right of persons, if one is deprived by theft or unjust damage of what is his, then the stolen goods must be returned to him to balance the scales of justice.

As a general rule, restitution should be made to the injured person, and it should be done as soon as is morally possible. For the injustice continues until the wrong has been righted. It is not necessary to make the restitution openly or in a way that would reveal the identity of the offending party. It can be made secretly or anonymously. For example, an employee who has stolen something from his employer can make restitution by doing extra work for which he is not paid.

How can restitution be made to someone whose identity is not known? Catholic moralists suggest giving the money or the goods to the poor, or to some worthy charity, or to the missions, since it can reasonably be presumed that that would be in accordance with the wishes of the injured party.

The obligation to restitution is a serious moral duty which should not be brushed off lightly. In fact, it is so serious that it also extends to all those who assist another to steal property from a third party. Thus, those who urge or counsel others to steal can be held to restitution; also those whose duty it is to prevent stealing, such as policemen, watchmen and employees of various kinds, when they help others steal by turning the other way can be held to restitution.

Restitution is a highly complex subject in Catholic moral theology. In difficult questions there are probably very few priests who can give good advice immediately in the confessional, without first consulting books on the subject or some qualified moral theologian. If the question ever comes up, try to find an experienced, prudent, learned priest who can help you out. Even he may not have the answer immediately to a complex question and may ask you to wait for an answer to your question so that he can consult the experts.

Finally, the Seventh Commandment has to do with the virtue of justice: to respect the property of others and to render to each person what is due to him or her. It seems to me that the Golden Rule applies here: "Do unto others as you would have them do unto you." If someone unjustly deprives another of his property, then he or she is held to restitution. Those are some of the basic truths contained in the Seventh Commandment: "You shall not steal."

COMMANDMENT 8: NO LYING

You shall not bear false witness against your neighbor.
(Exod. 20:16; Deut. 5:20)

The topic of today's sermon is the Eighth Commandment, "You shall not bear false witness against your neighbor." We find this Commandment in Exodus 20:16 and also in Matthew 5:33. This is an important topic today with the prominence of the mass media and the abundance of information that is spread throughout the world every day. Now when public figures are caught lying they usually do not admit that they lied; they say rather that they "misspoke." I think that means they said something not true, but imply that they did not do it deliberately. It is something like "I made a mistake."

A lie is a deception and there is a lot of that in our society. We see it in claims made for certain products and we see it in the financial crisis of that past few years. Another way of manipulating the truth is called "spinning." I am not sure what the definition of that is, but it is surely not clearly saying Yes to what is and No to what is not, as Our Lord teaches in the Gospel.

Everyone knows from his own conscience that lying is a sin. Lying is deception. It can be done by words or by a sign or by a gesture. A person lies when he says something he knows is not true—either by affirming something to be that does not exist, or by denying something that really does exist. So lying is forbidden by the natural law and also by divine revelation in the Ten Commandments.

In the Old Testament lying is considered an abomination. Thus, we read in the book of Sirach: "Lying is an ugly blot on a man, and ever on the lips of the ignorant. A thief is preferable to an inveterate liar, but both are heading for ruin. Lying is an abominable habit, so that disgrace is the liar's forever" (20:24–28).

The New Testament repeats the Eighth Commandment of the OT, but now the motivation has changed. The Christian should avoid all unrighteousness and all falsehood because he is a new creature in Christ Jesus. St. Paul summarizes this clearly in Ephesians (4:24–25): "Therefore, putting away falsehood, let every one speak the truth with his neighbor."

Since the time of the early Fathers of the Church, lying has been minutely analyzed by countless theologians and saints. That is because sins of the tongue are so common. The basic component of a lie is that someone deliberately says or communicates something that is contrary to what he or she thinks. Thus, if someone asks me, "Did you go to Mass today," and I reply, "Yes, I did," when in fact I did not, that is a lie, for it is a communication of something which is contrary to what I know to be a fact or to be true.

A lie is contrary to the truth. But what is truth? A famous Roman Governor in the Gospel asked that question. Truth is fundamentally a relationship of conformity between what is in the mind and reality that exists outside the mind. Speaking the truth is subject to the control of the human will. Since that conformity can be distorted in many different ways, the will needs to be trained and habituated to expressing only what it knows to be true. Such a habit is known as the virtue of truthfulness. We should all strive to develop the virtue of truthfulness because it is so easy for us to tell a lie in order to escape some difficulty.

The virtue of truthfulness is supremely important for the happiness of the individual and the good of human society, for it keeps the human mind in touch with external reality and it avoids all deceit, and all the evils which follow upon deceit, in human relationships. By being truthful a person is and becomes good in the moral order.

It is a fact that lying breaks down human relationships and is destructive of human society. When a husband and wife regularly lie to each other, there can be no communion of life between them. When a government lies to its people, the people learn to distrust everything that government does. St. Thomas Aquinas said that the truth is something that we owe to others—like a debt to be paid (STh II-II, 109, 3, ad 1).

Since lying is contrary to the natural moral law, it is never allowed. Thus, a deliberate lie is always a sin. In itself a lie, though intrinsically evil, is a venial sin. However, lying becomes mortally sinful if another virtue besides veracity (for example justice or charity) is thereby gravely violated. Accordingly, it is a mortal sin to tell al lie under oath or to deny one's Catholic faith.

Even though we may never tell a lie, there are times when we are bound in conscience to conceal the truth. For we are not obliged at all times to tell the whole truth. The reason for this is that secrets must be kept, and the good reputation of another can be ruined by revealing what is true about him but should not be made known. Some people ask a lot of questions and they have no right to the knowledge. One way to get around this problem is the use of what is known as a "mental reservation."

A mental reservation is had if the real meaning of the expression can be inferred from the circumstances of the question, or from customary usage, even if, as a matter of fact, such inference is not actually made. Thus, in answering the telephone or the door, to say that someone is not at home or "is not in," leaves open the reasonable inference that the person is not available "to you."

Mental reservations are morally permissible, sometimes even obligatory, provided there is a sufficient reason for using them and the questioner has no real right to know the truth. Thus, children cannot use them to their parents, since the parents have the right to know what their children are doing. But professional people, like doctors, lawyers, psychologists, who possess committed secrets from their clients, may use a mental reservation in order to protect their clients. So when asked an invasive question, they can reply "I do not know," that is, "I do not know anything that I may communicate to you." But such methods should be used sparingly. Truth is always the best policy and we should not veil it unless we really have sufficient reason to do so.

I once had a friend who constantly used mental reservations in normal conversation. Everyone knew it. The result was that his friends tended to discount all he said, since they could not be sure whether he was telling truth or offering some "hidden meaning."

Jesus and Mary are models of truthfulness. Jesus said of himself that he is "the truth." He said to Pontius Pilate: "For this I was born, and for this I have come into the world, to bear witness to the truth. Everyone who is of the truth hears my voice" (John 18:37). We should listen to that voice and speak the truth.

The Bible is full of admonitions to avoid falsehood and to speak the truth. Let me conclude with these strong words of St. James: "If any one thinks he is religious, and does not bridle his tongue but deceives his heart, this man's religion is vain. Religion that is pure and undefiled before God and the Father is this: to visit orphans and widows in their affliction, and to keep oneself unstained from the world" (James 1:26–27).

COMMANDMENTS 9 & 10: COVETING

You shall not covet your neighbor's house; you shall not covet your neighbor's wife, or his manservant, or his maidservant, or his ox, or his ass, or anything that is your neighbor's.

(Exod. 20:17; Deut. 5:21)

The last two Commandments are directed to man's mind and heart, that is, they concern the interior life of each person where thoughts and desires reign supreme. So God's law touches not just the exterior act but also the interior dimension of thinking and willing. A little reflection reveals that the Ninth Commandment is closely linked with the Sixth, and the Tenth relates to the Seventh. In the New Testament there is more emphasis on the interior life of man than there was in the Old Testament. For this reason Christianity has sometimes been called "ethical monotheism," that is, belief in one God with emphasis on man's mind and heart.

The Ninth Commandment is found in Deuteronomy 5:21: "You shall not covet your neighbor's wife." The word "covet" means: to wish for enviously, to desire inordinately or culpably. Thus, the Ninth Commandment tells us to be pure in thought and desire and it forbids all thoughts and desires contrary to the virtue of chastity.

On many occasions Jesus warned his disciples to avoid all unclean and wicked desires. One of the eight beatitudes also covers this matter: "Blessed are the pure in heart, for they shall see God" (Matt. 5:8). In another place Jesus says: "For out of the heart come evil thoughts, murders, adulteries, immorality, thefts, false witness, blasphemies. These are the things that defile a man" (Matt.15:19–20). So evil thoughts are forbidden by God because evil thoughts lead to evil deeds. A modern author summarized this truth by saying that "ideas have consequences."

St. Paul stressed the same idea: "Therefore mortify your members, which are on earth: immorality, uncleanness, lust, evil desire and covetousness (which is a form of idol-worship). Because of these things the wrath of God comes upon the unbelievers" (Col. 3:5–6). And St. Peter warns us in his first letter: "Beloved, I exhort you as strangers and pilgrims to abstain from carnal desires which war against the soul" (2:11).

Some Catholics seem to think that only external acts are sinful and that the law of God does not govern one's inner thoughts and desires. The above quotations from Scripture should show very clearly that that idea is false. However, a careful distinction should be made between evil thoughts that are spontaneous, unprovoked and unwilled and those that are deliberately willed and fostered. A sign of our fallen nature—that some of the effects of original sin are still with us—is that we do not have complete control over our thoughts and desires. This is called "concupiscence" or the persistence of evil desires contrary to our will.

Thus, sometimes evil thoughts come into our minds and we do not know where they come from or why—such as ideas of hatred or revenge, adulterous thoughts, impure desires, even blasphemous thoughts. It is very important to remember that such thoughts, no matter how evil or how persistent they might be, are not sinful as long as one does not give consent to them. When tormented by such thoughts we should have immediate recourse to prayer and also divert our attention to other good or harmless objects. This is the advice that the saints and the masters of the spiritual life have given for centuries.

Such thoughts about impure things become sinful when a person thinks of an unchaste act and deliberately takes pleasure in so thinking, or when unchaste desire or passion is aroused and consent is given to it. It should be clear that pornography in all its forms, especially on the Internet, because its purpose is to stimulate lustful desires and passions, is condemned and forbidden by the Ninth Commandment.

This commandment is very important today because of the many immodest images and lustful messages easily available in the omnipresent electronic media.

The Tenth Commandment is: "You shall not covet your neighbor's goods" (Deut. 5:21). God's Tenth "Word" applies the notion of "covetousness" to the realm of material possessions. It forbids all willful desires to take or to keep unjustly what belongs to others, and it also forbids envy at their success and good fortune. Please note that the Commandment covers such desires that are willed or fostered. If a person suddenly realizes that he is beset by such thoughts but has not deliberately consented to them, then there is no sin. As in the case of the Ninth Commandment, sin enters into the picture when one comes to the full realization of what one is doing, knows that it is sinful, but then deliberately persists in that activity. You may break one of God's laws at times without knowing it but that is not the same thing as committing a sin. You cannot commit a sin by chance or by accident or by not knowing what you are doing. Truly moral and responsible thoughts and actions must be freely willed; if they are not freely willed, they are not formal sins.

The Bible also warns us against greed and avarice: "Take heed and guard yourselves from all covetousness, for a man's life does not consist in the abundance of his possessions" (Luke 12:15). And again: "Money is the root of all evils, and some in their eagerness to get rich have strayed from the faith and have involved themselves in many troubles" (1 Tim. 6:10).

By means of the Ninth and Tenth Commandments the Lord is telling us to avoid all evil desires because they lead to evil deeds. This does not mean that our minds should be a vacuum. On the contrary, we should cultivate good and holy and healthy desires. If we do that consistently then we will be rewarded with both spiritual and psychological health. So the last two commandments have a negative and a positive side to them. On the one hand, they command us to avoid and reject evil desires regarding sexual matters—lusting after sexual pleasure outside of marriage; they command us to avoid and reject all greed and avarice regarding the possessions of others. On the other hand, there is a positive aspect of these Commandments—that we should have wholesome thoughts of charity and justice with regard to all, and to rejoice at the success and good fortune of others. We should pray that they use their abundance of goods to help others and for the praise and glory of God.

PRUDENCE

In previous sermons we have considered the three "theological virtues" – faith hope and charity. They are called "theological" because they have God as their object. The topic of our next four reflections will be the four "cardinal" virtues—prudence, justice, temperance and fortitude. They are called "cardinal" because they are HINGE virtues or KEY virtues which govern all the other moral virtues. They are called "moral" virtues because they have to do with free, human acts proceeding from man's mind and will. Moral virtues have to do with the means to the end, that is, human thoughts words, and deeds that are in conformity with right reason and God's will and put us on the road to our eternal destiny which is the face to face vision of God in heaven for all eternity.

A virtue is a habitual and firm disposition to do something good. It allows a person to perform good acts with ease and consistency. It is like knowing how to walk, to talk, to ride a bicycle, to brush your teeth and to tie your shoes. Man is a bundle of habits; Aristotle said that man is a habitual animal. Moral virtues have to do with human acts of an ethical nature which maintain good relations with God and with other persons. St. Gregory of Nyssa said that "The goal of a virtuous life is to become like God" (CCC 1803).

Prudence is the most important of the cardinal virtues because it guides all the other virtues. So when one acts with justice, temperance or fortitude he must do it <u>prudently</u>, otherwise he may go to extremes of either too much or too little. Thus, one who unnecessarily exposes himself to danger is not courageous but rash or foolhardy.

The word "prudence" is contracted from "providence" and means seeing ahead. St. Thomas says that prudence is "right reason in action" (S. Th. II-II, 47, 2). "Prudence is the virtue that disposes practical reason to discern our true good in every circumstance and to choose the right means of achieving it; 'the prudent man looks where he is going'" (CCC 1806). So to be prudent means to choose the right means to attain a good end, such as providing sufficient food for one's family, or for a student to study diligently in order to pass his examinations.

To say of someone that he is prudent is to praise him. Prudence is more characteristic of older people because of their experience of the joys and sorrows of human living. Youth are often lacking in prudence because of their lack of experience, so they often tend to act rashly and foolishly. The wisdom books in the Old Testament, like Proverbs and Sirach, praise prudence and warn us about the follies of youth. "With the help of this virtue we apply moral principles to particular cases without error and overcome doubts about the good to achieve and the evil to avoid" (CCC 1806).

There are two kinds or levels of prudence: a) naturally acquired human prudence, and b) divinely infused prudence. In their operation it is not easy to distinguish between the two. Human prudence is learned from experience on the natural level. Infused prudence is a special power we receive with Baptism and sanctifying grace. Here we are mainly concerned with the supernatural gift of the moral virtue of prudence. Fr. Jordan Aumann defines it thus: "It is a special virtue infused by God into the practical intellect for the right government of one's actions in view of the supernatural end" (*Spiritual Theology*, OSV, 1979, p. 276). So it is a) a gift from God, b) it has to do with the supernatural order or eternal salvation, c) it is an activity of reason enlightened by faith and informed with charity.

Prudence is the most necessary of all the moral virtues because it guides us in the choice of the right way to act in all circumstances; it guides us in the proper way to practice the theological virtues of faith, hope and charity, and the other moral virtues of justice, temperance and fortitude. Prudence helps us to avoid sin and to grow in virtue so that we can live as children of God. Prudence is important in the life of each individual. It is also essential for those who direct or command others, such as bishops, priests, spiritual directors, preachers, parents, teachers, employers, doctors and government officials.

In order to act prudently three mental acts are required: a) DELIBERATION. One must consider the various means to attain the end; he must know the principles that govern this case and have the ability to relate them to the concrete circumstances, such as always tell the truth; b) JUDGMENT: Once the matter has been considered, he must decide on the correct and lawful means to the end proposed; c) EXECUTION. The last step is for the will to command that the decision should be put into effect.

There are some characteristics, qualities or aspects of prudence that are listed by St. Thomas and by other masters of the spiritual life. Here we will consider just a few of them:

a. MEMORY OF THE PAST: We learn from past experience what to do and what to avoid in concrete circumstances in order to act well or virtuously.

b. UNDERSTANDING THE PRESENT: This is necessary in order to judge whether a given action is morally good or evil.

c. DOCILITY: This means that those who lack experience are willing to take advice from those who have experience and are already prudent.

d. REASONING POWER: If time permits, one should reflect on the principles involved and the particular circumstances before acting.

e. FORESIGHT: This means that one can see that the means chosen for the end are truly appropriate.

It is very helpful for young and old to have models of good Christian living to imitate, such as a favorite saint or holy person, such as St. Francis of Assisi, St. Theresà, or someone like Blessed Mother Teresa of Calcutta. It is also helpful to measure one's actions in terms of eternal salvation: for example, the Jesuit youth, Saint John Berchmans, constantly asked himself this question before every event: What has this to do with my eternal salvation?

As we make progress in the spiritual life we strive to conform our life to the will of God in all things; that will is made known to us by the Ten Commandments, by the teaching of the Church, and by the duties of my state in life. Another way of saying the same thing is that we strive to do all things for the glory of God. We should always remain open to the inspirations of the Holy Spirit which is the gift of counsel. The gift of counsel is closely related to the virtue of prudence—and actually goes beyond it. Perhaps a good example of this is when Mother Teresa, on a train ride in India, saw clearly that God wanted her to leave her religious teaching order after twenty years and to occupy herself with caring for the poor. She went on to found the Missionaries of Charity who now care for the poor on all five continents.

One who has the virtue of prudence is a person who has good judgment about choosing the right means to attain a good end. St. Thomas says it is right reason in action. We all look to older people for guidance in difficult matters because they have experience and often can tell us what to do in difficult circumstances and what to avoid. This is the fruit of a long life—it is the fruit of failure and success in the trials and tribulations of human existence.

To lead a good Christian life it is necessary to have the moral virtue of prudence. Without it one will fall victim to error and mortal sin. The prudent person is the one who knows the will of God and strives to fulfill it in all aspects of his life. The prudent person is the one who is on the road to eternal life, with his eyes, mind and heart fixed on the goal. Let us pray today for an increase of divine grace and for a share in that prudence which is a quality of the children of God who are on the road to eternal salvation.

JUSTICE

The four moral virtues that are given to us by God at our Baptism, along with divine grace and the three theological virtues of faith, hope and charity, are prudence, justice temperance and fortitude. We have already considered the virtue of prudence and how important it is for our whole spiritual life. Today I would like to say a few things about the virtue of justice.

In recent decades we have heard a lot of talk about justice: justice for the poor, for minorities, for the handicapped, and so forth. Justice is often linked with "peace," because peace is the result of justice. However, the secular understanding of justice is very different from that of the Church. In secular language it is often meant in a socialist or Marxian sense.

Everyone knows what justice means: It means rendering to each person what is due to him. Justice is important in both personal and social life. It puts things in their right order and so leads to peace, which St. Augustine said is "the tranquility of order." To be a just person means to refrain from doing any evil to others, and to do the good to others that they deserve. This involves such things as paying one's debts, respecting the property of others, driving safely, showing respect for others, and so forth. So justice is a way of carrying out the first principle of the moral order—to do good and to avoid evil. It has special relevance to respecting the property of others and to honor their good name.

Philosophers and moral theologians distinguish justice on three levels: a) our obligations to the state, such as paying just taxes and serving in the military if necessary; b) the obligation of the state to each individual, that is, not showing favoritism and treating everyone as equal before the law; c) the rights and duties of individual persons among themselves; this has to do with honesty and fairness in our dealings with others, especially with the members of our own family. This type of justice is called "commutative justice" and is the most important of the three because it affects many of our words and actions each day since we are by nature social animals.

Here are some of the characteristics of a truly just person.

—He treats others with respect and honesty and sees the image of God in them; he is always polite in dealing with others.

—He does not contract debts without necessity, and he pays his debts on time.

—He treats the possessions of others, and public property, as carefully as his own property.

—He does not damage the good name of others by gossip, detraction or calumny.

There are other virtues related to justice that are called its parts. Here I would like to mention a few of them. The first and most important one is the virtue of RELIGION which inclines us to give to God the worship due him as the first principle of all things and as our Creator.

RELIGION has both an internal and an external aspect. INTERNAL: The internal acts of religion are DEVOTION and PRAYER. Devotion, or being a devout Catholic, means that one has love for God and strives to obey him in all things. Prayer means raising the mind and heart to God and engaging in intimate conversation with him about the problems of daily life. EXTERNAL: The main external acts of religion are adoration and sacrifice. ADORATION means showing external respect for God, avoiding taking God's name in vain and avoiding blasphemy. SACRIFICE is the main external and public worship of God. The supreme sacrifice is that of Jesus on the Cross on Calvary which is re-presented at each offering of Mass. Sacrifice means to remove some good, some valuable thing from our control and to offer it to God; we do this when we deny ourselves some food, drink or entertainment during Lent. So RELIGION is the most important part of justice because of its object, namely, giving to God our Creator what is due to him, since everything we have, except our sins, comes from him and his bounty.

Other virtues that are related to justice are the following:

1. OBEDIENCE: We owe obedience to all lawful authorities, such as parents, teachers, pastor, employer, just laws passed by the state. This is very difficult because it means bending our will to the will of others. But we recognize the hand of God in authority; Jesus said that all authority comes from God.

2. GRATITUDE: This is related to justice; it means sincerely acknowledging benefits received from others by thanking them and returning the favor at some time in the future.

3. VERACITY or telling the truth. One should always manifest externally what one is thinking and not try to deceive others. One can never lie, but one must sometimes conceal the truth by silence or by some kind of mental reservation.

4. Closely related to the virtue of JUSTICE is the gift of PIETY from the Holy Spirit. The gift of PIETY is a supernatural habit, which moves the will, through the aid of the Holy Spirit, to show a filial love for God the Father, and a sentiment of universal love for all men and women as our brothers and sisters and as children of the same heavenly Father. Here the emphasis is more on God as our loving Father than as the omnipotent Creator of heaven and earth. So this gift of the Holy Spirit helps us to develop the virtue of justice in our relations with God and our neighbor.

An outstanding model of the virtue of justice and one we can imitate is Joseph, the husband of Mary and foster father of Jesus. St. Matthew says that Joseph was "a just man." This means that he was a very holy man who obeyed God in all things and showed love for others (Matt. 1:19). In his life he illustrates everything said above about the moral virtue of justice.[1]

----

1. Source consulted in preparing this sermon: Jordan Aumann, O.P., *Spiritual Theology* (OSV, 1979).

TEMPERANCE

The four moral virtues, or cardinal virtues, which are infused with sanctifying grace at Baptism are prudence, justice, temperance and fortitude. Since they are associated with grace, they are supernatural virtues which are a special gift of God. Virtues are good habits which enable us to do good and to seek what is good. But vices are bad habits which lead us to do and seek what is evil, what is sinful. These four virtues are called "cardinal" from the Latin word "cardo" which means "hinge." This means that they are key virtues on which other virtues depend, just as a door depends on or hangs on its hinges. In order to attain eternal life and the face to face vision of God, we have to do good and to avoid evil; we have to practice love of God and love of neighbor. This means, in the practical order, that we must live a virtuous life. So the practice of virtue is absolutely necessary for us to reach the end or purpose for which God made us in the first place. I have already spoken to you about prudence and justice. Today I propose to say a few words about the virtue of TEMPERANCE.

When we hear the word "temperance" we know that it has something to do with moderation. Because of Original Sin, which we all inherit from Adam and Eve, our passions are not under the complete control of our reason. We are afflicted with what the theologians call "concupiscence." This means that our passions want to go their own way and resist the control of reason. Thus, the desire for food may be out of control so that one eats too much ice cream or candy; a special problem here is the abuse of alcoholic beverages. The temperate person also avoids all mind-altering drugs such as marijuana, cocaine, heroin, and so forth. The sexual instinct is difficult to control and can lead one to acts of impurity, adultery, fornication, sodomy, looking at pornography in magazines or on the Internet. In both of these cases, it is a matter of excess. Food and drink are good and necessary to sustain life, but they must be taken in moderation. Sex is good and is necessary for the continuation of the human race, but it was designed by God for the generation of children, not for entertainment, and is restricted to the married state.

The virtue of TEMPERANCE has to do with sense of taste, food and drink, and the sense of touch, sexual activity. Temperance, therefore, is the virtue which moderates in us the INORDINATE desire for sensible pleasure. Failure to be moderate in the use of food, drink and sex leads to many serious sins, breaks up families, and can easily lead to eternal damnation of individuals because of immersion in many mortal sins. Bad habits in these areas are difficult to correct, as we see in the case of alcoholics and those addicted to pornography and the related sexual sins.

Temperance is a Cardinal or Hinge virtue because other virtues related to the moderation of the passions depend on it or are applications of temperance in various areas of human living. Thus, moderation in eating food is a basic application of temperance. This means that one should not eat too much, or too little, as some teenagers do and get sick or die from anorexia. Moderation in drink means that one should not drink too much soda or any beverage, especially alcoholic beverages. Temperance with regard to alcoholic drinks is called "sobriety."

With regard to the sense of touch, the virtues related to Temperance are such things as chastity, purity and continence. Chastity moderates the desire for venereal pleasure. The use of the sexual function is restricted to those who are married. For those who are not married, the Sixth Commandment prohibits the use and enjoyment of the sexual powers.

The virtue of purity moderates the external acts that of their nature lead to, and prepare for, sexual union. So the pure single person avoids such things as passionate kissing, petting, and pornography of any kind. This virtue should be practiced by all, but in the months before the wedding especially by those who are engaged to be married.

The virtue of continence strengthens the will in order to resist the disordered vehemence of the passions and this is a virtue for both the married and the single person. When I was a teenager in St. Leo's Parish in Tacoma, Washington, every summer there would be a Sunday sermon on modesty. We don't hear much about that any more. We live in a culture that relishes and glorifies immodesty. But modesty, as a part of temperance, is important for our own spiritual good and also by not being the occasion of sins on the part of others. Basically, modesty is a virtue by which we observe proper decorum in our gestures and bodily movements, in our posture, and in the matter of dress. This applies to both men and women, but especially to women in summer time and hot weather. Immodesty of dress at Sunday Mass during the summer is a constant problem for many parishes, especially those near resort areas.

Temperance also covers playing and recreation activities. (St. Thomas calls it "eutrapelia," STh II-II, 168, aa.2–4.) Such activities should be wholesome, and should avoid anything that is sinful or excessive with regard to persons, places, times and other circumstances. This pertains to such things as watching TV, playing sports, attending plays and sporting events like baseball, football, basketball, hockey; it applies to hiking, swimming, playing games, such as video games, and so forth.

God made us for himself so he is our final end. We are all going to die, and when we die we hope to go to heaven. In order to get there, we must live a virtuous life now. This means that some things we must do, and some things we must avoid. We should avoid all occasions of sin that stimulate the desire for inordinate sensate pleasure, such as immoral films, TV programs, and Internet pornography. To lead a virtuous life we must practice self-control. It is for this reason that the Church recommends occasional fasting and abstinence from meat on Fridays, so we can learn self-control regarding sense pleasures.

We must practice "custody of the eyes" and control over our imagination and "day dreaming." It is a good idea to occupy oneself with some beneficial activities, like a hobby and physical exercise. As Catholics, we should cultivate a sense of Christian dignity. We should realize that, when we are in the state of grace, the Holy Trinity dwells in our souls, and that we are called to bear witness to Christ by giving good example to everyone we meet.

The virtue of Temperance is most important for remaining a friend of God, but often it is difficult to practice because of the vehemence of our passions. St. Paul tells us to pray always. In the Church we have the outstanding models of temperance in the saints, especially in our Blessed Mother and in St. Joseph. They are always ready to help us if we have the humility to ask for their intercession.[2]

---

2. Sources consulted in preparing this sermon: Jordan Aumann, O.P., *Spiritual Theology* (OSV, 1979); Gabriel of St. Mary Magdalen, O.C.D., *Divine Intimacy* (TAN, 1996).

FORTITUDE

Everyone admires bravery and courage in the face of danger. We see many examples of courage portrayed in films and TV programs. Often they have to do with situations of war, but there are also many examples of courage in the face of persecution, sickness or some kind of handicap, such as blindness or lameness.

We have already considered three of the cardinal virtues which are infused with sanctifying grace—prudence, justice and temperance. The fourth infused cardinal virtue is called "fortitude" or courage. Fortitude is a special supernatural virtue, given to us by God, to strengthen us so that we will not abandon the pursuit of the difficult good, even when faced with grave danger to bodily health and life. Here we are speaking of fortitude as a supernatural virtue that helps us to overcome difficulties and dangers to life and limb, and also that helps us to persevere in doing good, keeping God's Commandments, and striving to do his will in our daily life. Fortitude is located in what the philosophers call the "irascible" appetite or passion; this is the source of anger and, under the control of reason, moves us to defend ourselves against attacks that threaten our life or honor or possessions.

Fortitude also influences all the other virtues in the sense that we must be consistent and firm in striving for virtue and striving to obey God in all things, in spite of temptations from the world, the flesh and the devil. That is not an easy thing to do, and fidelity here requires help from the grace of God. He offers us that grace in the infused virtues and also in the Seven Gifts of the Holy Spirit. So fortitude is a special supernatural virtue that gives us moral strength so that we will not abandon the pursuit of the difficult good, even when faced with grave danger to bodily health or life, or when faced with a moral threat of committing a mortal sin, such as overindulgence in alcohol or in sexual sins of various kinds.

Fortitude functions in two ways: a) aggression or attack, and b) endurance of some kind of evil. Aggression is often exercised in war, when a soldier attacks the enemy with danger to his life; it is also exercised in attacking moral evils such as pornography. Endurance of evil is much more common. This takes place when a person is afflicted with some evil that cannot be avoided, such as a person dying from cancer or having open heart surgery, or living with migraine headaches or any other kind of permanent pain. There are many stories of bravery on the part of American servicemen who were captured by the Vietnamese communists and tortured. Two men come to mind – John McCain and Admiral Jeremiah Denton, both of whom came home as heroes and went on to serve in the U.S. Senate.

It is important to remember that the virtue of fortitude is "supernatural" and that it is given to us by God when we are baptized and as long as we remain in the state of grace. When a person falls into mortal sin, he loses charity, sanctifying grace and the moral virtues, but he does not lose faith and hope unless he sins against those virtues by apostasy or despair.

Some good examples of models in the practice of fortitude are: a) Jesus in his passion and Mary at the foot of the Cross; b) The Apostles. During Jesus' passion they were fearful and ran away, but after Pentecost when they had received the gift of the Holy Spirit, they were fearless proclaimers of the Gospel and died as martyrs for the faith; c) The North American martyrs – St. Isaac Jogues and St. Jean de Brebeuf; d) In our own time we have the example of Popes John Paul II, Benedict, XVI, Mother Teresa of Calcutta, Mother Angelica of EWTN, and Fr. Paul Marx, founder of Human Life International. Then there was that saintly man, Cardinal Ignatius Kung, Archbishop of Shanghai, China, who was kept in solitary confinement for 26 years. He said that three things kept him sane: daily meditation, the Rosary and daily exercise of Kung Fu. Eventually he was freed and he came to America.

The four Cardinal Virtues all have other virtues related to them that are expressions of fortitude in various areas of human existence. Here I will mention two other virtues that share in fortitude. A virtue we all need, and one that is very important, is the virtue of PATIENCE. Each day we encounter things that irritate us and that go contrary to our own wishes. The opposition may come from our own weaknesses or from things that other persons do that annoy us. "The virtue of patience enables us to bear physical and moral sufferings without sadness of spirit or dejection of heart" (Aumann, *Spiritual Theology*, p. 308). Some attitudes that help us practice patience are the following: a) seeking to conform ourselves to the loving will of God; b) making reparation for our sins in this life so we will not have to do it in purgatory; c) remembering the sufferings of Jesus and Mary and the great saints; d) the hope of pleasing God and building up merits for eternal life and eternal happiness with God.

The second virtue I want to mention here is PERSEVERANCE. This virtue inclines us to persist in the practice of the good in spite of the difficulties involved. We need a sense of perseverance in order to practice virtue over a long period of time. No matter how holy a person may be, he or she remains free and can still commit a mortal sin. For that reason we also need, over and above the virtue of perseverance, the special grace of final perseverance that the Council of Trent calls "a great gift." The grace of final perseverance means that a person dies in the state of sanctifying grace and so is assured of his eternal salvation and entrance into heaven.

On the positive side, there is also a virtue called "magnanimity." This is a Latin word which means "greatness of soul" or we might call it having a big heart. The magnanimous person is one who undertakes great acts worthy of honor. It is just the opposite of mediocrity. Many of the saints were magnanimous and accomplished great things for God. Think of the founders of religious orders such as St. Benedict, St. Francis of Assisi, St. Dominic, St. Ignatius Loyola, and many others. In our own time we have the example of Mother Teresa of Calcutta, and Mother Angelica who founded EWTN, the only worldwide Catholic TV network.

You have heard of the Seven Gifts of the Holy Spirit which strengthen and assist the infused theological and moral virtues; one of them is called "fortitude." The gift of Fortitude assists and strengthens the virtue of fortitude; it provides invincible

CONFIDENCE of overcoming any dangers or difficulties that may arise. The gift is a kind of instinctive interior impulse that proceeds directly from the Holy Spirit. The distinction between the virtue of fortitude and the gift of fortitude is the CONFIDENCE one experiences in being able to overcome dangers and difficulties.

It is not easy to lead a moral, Christian life constantly—to avoid sin and to practice virtue, especially in keeping the Commandments of God and rules of the Church. To do that we need courage and perseverance. God will give us those helps if we ask him for them. He is inviting all of us to be his friends. So we should pray every day and beg God for the grace of fortitude and perseverance in grace to our dying breath.

DEATH

From a very early age we all know what death is. We have seen plants die; we have seen animals die. We know, as it were instinctively, that life is fragile. Talking about death is not a popular subject for discussion at social gatherings, except perhaps for the brief statement that someone has "passed away," a very common euphemism for the harsh, cold reality of death. In personal conversation and even letters I have noticed that most people avoid using the word "death." I think the reason for this is that most people do not want to be reminded of the fact and the certitude of death.

Today I am going to violate that convention of speech, and talk explicitly about death. I want you to think about it seriously, since it concerns each one of us. It can happen to any one of us any day or night—we are all headed for death, either sooner or later.

But what is death? One definition is that death is the cessation of life by the separation of the soul from the body. By "soul" I mean the principle of life in a plant, an animal or man. Some of the signs of death are: cessation of movement, cessation of breathing, radical dismemberment, corruption of the flesh. Death means the end of human life in the flesh as we know it. All of us, with the exception of some young children, have had the experience of loved ones or friends dying. They are no more. Their bodies are buried in the ground; we can visit the cemetery and view the spot and headstone where their bodies were buried.

Death is a sad reality. And there is something in us which says that things should not be that way. We instinctively resist death and all that it implies. Old people who are soon to die, spend most of their time just trying to stay alive and to delay the moment of death. They spend lots of money on doctors and medicine to delay the certain eventual arrival of death. The Bible and the Church teach that death is a punishment for sin. St. Paul said, "The wages of sin is death" (Rom. 6:23). He also wrote, "... it is appointed unto men once to die, and after this the judgment" (Hebr. 9:27). The Council of Trent said that by his sin Adam became subject to death and transmitted death to all of his descendants (DS 1511ff.).

Because man is composed of material parts that can be separated, he is by nature mortal, just as all other living material beings are mortal. But in the beginning, as we know from the Bible, God endowed Adam and Eve in Paradise with the preternatural gift of bodily immortality. Thus, in their original state, they were exempted from the universal law of death. As punishment for their sin of disobedience to a divine command, however, they were made subject to the death that God had warned them about. For God has warned them: "Of the tree of the knowledge of good and evil you are not to eat, for on the day you eat of it you shall most surely die" (Gen 2:17). And in the next chapter we read: "With sweat on your brow shall you eat your bread, until you return to the soil, as you were taken from it. For dust you are and to dust you shall return" (3:19).

St. Paul teaches very clearly that death is a result of Adam's sin: "As through one man sin entered into the world and through sin death, and thus death has passed into all men because all have sinned" (Rom. 5:12). But for those who die in the state of sanctifying grace death is not so much a punishment as it is a consequence of sin. Since Our Lord and his Blessed Mother were free from original sin, death for them was not a result of sin; it was rather a consequence of life in a material body.

The law of death is universal. According to Genesis, St. Paul and the Council of Trent, all human beings, as descendants of Adam and Eve, are subject to Original Sin (excluding Jesus and Mary); therefore they are all subject to the law of death. This teaching is based especially on Romans 5:12ff. St. Paul also says in Hebrews 9:27, "It is appointed to men once to die and after that comes judgment."

Human life on this earth is a time of trial, temptation and merit. Death is the dividing line. During life one can perform good or evil deeds; one can merit eternal life or lose it; one can be a sinner for a time, like St. Augustine, and then go through a conversion. With death these kinds of changes cease. As one is at the moment of death, so one remains for all eternity. There is no possibility for merit or sin for those in heaven; there is no possibility of repentance and conversion for those in hell. Contrary views have been repeat-edly condemned by the Church. Thus, those in hell cannot attain heaven, just as those in heaven cannot sin and so lose their blessed state of union with God. We find confirmation of this truth in many places in the Bible. For example, Paul says: "For all the truth about us will be brought out in the law court of Christ, and each of us will get what he deserves for the things he did in the body, good or bad" (2 Cor. 5:10; see also Matt. 25:34ff; Luke 16:26; John 9:4).

It is excellent spiritual advice to prepare ourselves for death. There is an old saying that there are only two things in life that are absolutely certain: death and taxes. For some it may be possible to avoid taxes, but no one can avoid death. All the great and famous people we learned about in history classes are dead. The best preparation for death is a life of virtue. This means seeking God's will in all things and embracing that will. This means keeping the Ten Commandments. This means receiving the Sacraments of the Church, especially the Holy Eucharist and penance, on a regular basis as often as one can. This means coming in contact with God every day in prayer; it means to practice some self-denial in imita-tion of Jesus and helping others; in short, to practice love of God and love of neighbor. Anyone who does that is living a life of faith, hope and charity. Such a person leads a life of peace and joy because he has solid hope of attaining heaven.

Now is the acceptable time. Now is the day of salvation. We must provide for our eternal salvation by our own efforts while we have the time, and not rely on others. Many saints and spiritual authors recommend that we think about death every day, because we might not live to see another day. This helps us to focus on why we are here in this life and what our ultimate destiny is—the face to face vision of God for all eternity.

The wise person provides for the future. It is an act of divine wisdom and a sign of prudence to be ready to meet the Lord when he comes to call us to himself. It could happen any day and will certainly happen on a day in the future that is unknown to us.

THE LAST JUDGMENT

In the sermon on death I mentioned the Church teaching about the "particular judgment" that takes place immediately after death, when the soul leaves the body. Jesus is our judge and each person knows immediately whether he is going to heaven, to purgatory or to hell. This judgment is individual and personal and irreversible. Scripture, however, is very emphatic in asserting that there is also a general or last judgment of all mankind at the end of the world. In that dread moment, the dead will rise from their graves, Christ will come again in glory and all will stand before Jesus Christ, the eternal Judge, to await his decision.

Belief in the General or Last Judgment is an integral part of the Catholic faith. It is present in both the Apostles' Creed and the Nicene Creed which we pray every Sunday. They profess that Christ now "sits at the right hand of God the Father almighty and will come again in glory to judge the living and the dead" when the world comes to its end.

In the Gospels Jesus frequently speaks about the "day of judgment." He gives his listeners, including us, plenty of advance warning. He assures us that he will execute judgment: "For the Son of Man is going to come in the glory of his Father with his angels, and, when he does, he will reward each one according to his behavior" (Matt. 16:27). The Father has handed over all judgment to the Son: "The Father judges no one; he has entrusted all judgment to the Son, so that all may honor the Son as they honor the Father.... The Father... has appointed him supreme judge because he is the Son of Man" (John 5:22–27).

St. Peter affirms of Jesus that "God has appointed him to judge everyone, alive or dead" (Acts 10:42). St. Paul makes the same point when he says: "According to the good news I preach, God, through Jesus Christ, judges the secrets of mankind" (Rom. 2:16). St. John describes the final judgment in terms of rendering an account of all one's deeds which are written down in a book.

The examination of deeds written in a book is meant to be an image or symbol of a spiritual or mental process that takes place all at once, in an instant, because of the omniscience and almighty power of God who knows all things and can do all things (see Rev. 20:11–15).

Jesus paints a vivid, memorable picture of the last judgment in the parable found in Matthew 25:31–46. The Son of Man, escorted by his angels, will take his seat on the throne of glory. "All the nations will be assembled before him and he will separate men one from another as the shepherd separates sheep from goats. He will place the sheep on his right hand and the goats on his left" (verses 32–33). The basis of his judgment will be how generously people responded to the needs of others during their lifetime. Jesus identified himself with those people and their needs. "Just as you did not do it to one of the least of these, you did not do it to me" (Matt. 25:45). The same idea was expressed by Jesus when he appeared to Saul on the road to Damascus. Saul was persecuting Christians and when he fell to the ground at the sight of the glorified Christ, Jesus said to him, "Saul, Saul, why do you persecute me?" (Acts 9:4).

While the particular judgment is individual and personal, the general judgment answers to the social side of man's nature. So on the last day we will be judged not only as individuals, but also as members of society. In this way God will reveal to all his justice in those he condemns and his mercy in those who are saved.

There is also the matter of the body sharing in the final reward or punishment. The saved and the damned after they have died, at the present time and until the end of the world, do not have their bodies. But at the general judgment, when they have risen from the dead and the body is rejoined to the soul, the body will share in the final punishment or reward.

Another reason for the final judgment is that a full and public verdict with regard to each person cannot be reached while history is still running its course. Both our good deeds and our evil deeds can and do have far-reaching effects. For example, the good example of St. Francis of Assisi still motivates many people to imitate his virtue. Bishop Fulton J. Sheen is still converting men and women to Christ through his books, talks and videos. Parents live on in their children; how they have raised them affects others. Pornographers, who write books and make films to lead others into sexual sins, will be held accountable for the sins caused by their works even after they have died. So only on the last day, when all of our deeds have attained their final effect, can a truly definitive judgment be made.

At the last judgment nothing will escape the notice of the Eternal Judge. He will judge us on the basis of our good deeds and our evil deeds, on our external actions and the desires of our hearts. As with the Second coming of Jesus and the resurrection of the dead, no one knows, except our Father in heaven, when the general judgment will take place. According to St. Thomas Aquinas, it is very probable that the judgment will be in the form of a spiritual or mental enlightenment of all and will take place in an instant. We should not imagine it to be like a series of trials in a courtroom, one after the other, with documents and lawyers, going through the billions of human beings who have walked on this earth. God will make known immediately, and to all, the merits and the demerits of each person.

Where will the last judgment take place? We do not know for certain from what we find in the Bible. The prophet Joel speaks of the "Valley of Jehosaphat" (Joel 4) as the place of judgment. This is the area around Jerusalem and near the Mount of Olives where Jesus ascended into heaven. Perhaps it is to be understood symbolically, but St. Thomas thinks it probable that Jesus will return in glory to the earth at the same place where he ascended into heaven forty days after his resurrection on the Mount of Olives in Jerusalem.

God has not revealed to us when the world will end, but it is absolutely certain that human history on this earth will come to an end at the time appointed by God. There will be no more being born and dying. All will be assigned to either heaven or hell according to their merits. It will happen suddenly. Our Lord tells us to be prepared at all times, for his coming will not be announced ahead of time. As he said, he will come like a thief in the night when one least expects it.

Therefore we must always be prepared for the coming of the Lord, whether it is for our own death or for the end of the world. His word to us is: Watch and pray. We do that by each day raising our mind and heart to God, by keeping his commandments, and by receiving his sacraments as often as we can. If we persevere in that, we will meet him with joy as our loving Savior who will welcome us into paradise to be with him forever. Amen.

HEAVEN

Everyone wants to be happy. And what is it that makes us happy? It is the possession of good things that we desire—a tasty meal, a new suit of clothes, a good night's sleep, the acquisition of a new house—the list is endless. But the problem with human happiness is that none of these things completely satisfies the human heart. They are all fragile and can easily be lost. And everything that one acquires in this life is taken away with death, which is always just around the corner and ready to knock on our door. In other words, man seeks permanent, complete happiness, but he cannot find it in this life. Does this mean that man will always be frustrated? By no means.

The Christian answer to this problem is the promise of eternal life with God in heaven. Jesus tells us that man cannot find complete happiness in this life, but only in God who is our Creator, Redeemer and Sanctifier. God is by his nature infinite goodness and life and he wills to share that eternal life with those who obey him, love him, and die as his friend, endowed with sanctifying grace and the theological virtues of faith, hope and charity. What each person really desires is perfect happiness without end and that can be found only in God. Finding perfect, permanent happiness is what we mean by the word "heaven." Today I would like to offer few insights on what the Church teaches about heaven.

Heaven can be defined as the place and condition of perfect supernatural happiness. It is a "place" because Jesus and Mary are there with their resurrected bodies, even though it is not the same kind of place we inhabit. It is also a "condition" because it involves a modification of the human mind and will so that we can see and love God directly, without having to use material images as we now do. In our present situation when we are immersed in space and time, heaven seems very mysterious to us. It is impossible to imagine what it might be like. St. Paul, who was granted a brief glimpse of heaven, says: "Eye has not seen, nor ear heard, nor has it entered into the heart of man what things God has prepared for those that love him" (1 Cor. 2:9).

The Church's teaching on heaven is very consoling. She says that the souls of the just that in the moment of death are free from all guilt of sin and free from the punishment due to sin (that is, if they do not have to go to purgatory first) enter immediately into heaven. We profess our belief in this revealed truth when we pray the Apostles' Creed, "I believe... in life everlasting," and when we profess in the Creed at Sunday Mass, "I look for the resurrection of the dead, and the life of the world to come." These expressions, "life everlasting" and "the life of the world to come" are synonyms for "heaven."

Heaven, as a place and condition of eternal happiness, is often referred to by most people even in daily conversation; the words "heaven" and "hell" and the realities behind them keep cropping up in our conversation in various ways—seriously or thoughtlessly or merely in jest. This shows, it seems to me, that the possibility of eternal happiness or eternal suffering is often on the minds of most people. This is so because we are all concerned about our future, and all adults know that their present life will end, sooner or later.

Our knowledge about the reality of heaven has been revealed to us by God and it finds expression in the Bible, especially in the New Testament. In the Gospels Jesus speaks clearly about heaven. He vividly paints the happiness of heaven by comparing it to a wedding feast, at which there is an abundance of food, wine, music and dancing (see Matt. 25:10) and he calls it "eternal life." According to St. John, one attains life everlasting through the knowledge of God and Christ: "Eternal life is this: to know you, the only true God, and Jesus Christ whom you have sent" (John 17:3).

St. John the Apostle stresses in several places in his writings that one attains eternal life or heaven by believing in Jesus, the Messiah and Son of God (see John 3:16; 20:31; 1 John 5:13). He also says that eternal life consists in conformity to God, and in the direct vision of God: "We shall be like him because we shall see him as he really is" (1 John 3:2).

The basic human acts which are involved in happiness in heaven are <u>knowledge,</u> <u>love</u> and <u>joy;</u> eternal happiness does not consist in eating, drinking, possessions and engaging in sexual activity. The mind and heart of man will be totally satisfied and rejoice in the direct knowledge and love of God. Love and friendship is what all men seek and that desire is perfectly fulfilled in heaven.

Many Catholics wonder about whether or not they will know their parents, relatives and friends in heaven. On this point most Catholic theologians have taught that the blessed in heaven, in addition to the vision of God, also enjoy the companionship of their loved ones who are also in heaven. At the present time there is something lacking in the happiness of the saints in heaven, that is, the saints have not yet been reunited to their bodies. That will take place at the end of the world when all will rise from the dead, Christ will come again in glory, and the General Judgment will occur.

Some people wonder whether or not there can be a change in the status of those in heaven and in hell. In other words, can the blessed in heaven commit sin and so lose their eternal happiness? In the early Church some theologians thought that they could change, but the Church has consistently condemned that idea. In fact, in a solemn dogmatic statement Pope Benedict XII in the 14th century declared: "The vision and this enjoyment (of the Divine Essence) continues without interruption or diminution of the vision and enjoyment, and will continue until the general judgment and thenceforth for all eternity" (DS 1000). Those who attain heaven, therefore, can never lose that blessed state; they cannot sin as man in this life can and be rejected by God. St. Thomas Aquinas gives the reason for this: Man seeks infinite good and finds it only in God in heaven; since he is confirmed in good by the vision of God, his will cannot prefer anything else to God because there is nothing else. Thus Jesus compares the reward for good works with treasures in heaven which cannot be lost (Matt. 6:20; Luke 12:33); and St. Paul calls eternal happiness in heaven "an incorruptible crown" (1 Cor. 9:25).

Another question about heaven is whether or not there is equality of vision. Yes, all are happy, but are some of the saints more happy or closer to God than others? The Church has given a clear answer to this question. It is a dogmatic, infallible teaching of the Catholic Church that the level of participation in the Beatific Vision granted to the saved is proportioned to each one's merits. For, the Council of Florence in the 15th century declared that the saved "see clearly the Triune God himself, just as he is, some more perfectly than others according to their respective merits" (DS 1304–1306). Thus, Jesus promised that he will "render to everyone according to his works" (Matt. 16:27). In the same vein St. Paul writes that "each will duly be paid according to his share in the work" (1 Cor. 3:8). Also, Jesus' words about the many "rooms" or "mansions" in his Father's house have often been interpreted, in Catholic tradition, as affirming the inequality of rewards, depending on each one's merits (see John 14:2).

Belief in heaven, therefore, gives us a powerful motive to try to gain as much merit as we can, now, while we have time to worship God, to grow in virtue and to practice the love of God and love of neighbor. These are the "good works" that build up for us our "treasure in heaven."

HELL

I know it is not popular these days to speak about Hell, but it is a fact of our religion and divine revelation. Its existence and eternal duration are defined dogmas of the Church. It is indeed strange, isn't it? The modern mind rejects the very notion of Hell and makes a joke out of it—you know, the red devil with his long tail and three-pronged spear—but the word "Hell" is used very often and casually by many people in daily conversation. This is characteristic of the secularism, atheism and materialism of our pagan culture. The notion of Hell involves something final, irrevocable: absolute rejection, total despair. The secular mind runs away from that and rejects the very possibility, because it denies the absolute value of truth and has embraced a philosophy of relativism.

Reflecting on Hell is very sobering for our faith and our love of Jesus. It reminds us that we could deny him and reject him for all eternity, with the result that he rejects us. We should beware of the current naive optimism that all will be saved, or according to the *New Oxford Review*, "that all will sail off to heaven in a pink sailboat." An old Jesuit friend of mine, who was a counselor and retreat master for many nuns and priests, told me one time that he never omitted the meditation on Hell in retreats to priests or nuns, assuming that they do not need it because they are beyond that; we all need it.

There is much help for our imagination in the passage in St. Luke about the Rich Man and Lazarus. Hell is mentioned often in the New Testament— about thirty times. St. Teresa of Avila was shown, in a vision, the place in Hell reserved for her, if she did not correspond to God's grace. The children of Fatima were shown a vision of Hell that terrified them. Origen's "apocatastasis omnium" (restoration of all) has been condemned many times in the past, that is, that the punishment of devils and human persons in Hell is only temporary and that, eventually, all will attain heaven.

In this reflection we should try to use our imagination, memory and senses to enter into the sense of pain, despair, and utter loneliness of the damned. You might try to get inside the hearts and minds and bodies of the damned to see and experience as best you can how they feel. Note how all creation has turned against them, since they have turned against the Creator of all of them. We are all one heartbeat from purgatory, heaven, or hell.

Imagine the cries and blasphemies against Christ our Lord and against his saints. Since this is a place of total and absolute despair and hatred, perhaps you can imagine the cries of anguish, the cursing, blasphemies directed against Christ our Lord, his Blessed Mother, the saints, and also against you. There is nothing but hatred here. There is NO HOPE!

Similar hatred was shown to Pope John Paul II during his visit to Holland in the 1980s; against Cardinal Ratzinger when he lectured in New York in January 1988; also by the homosexuals against Cardinal O'Connor in St. Patrick's Cathedral on December 9, 1989.

With the sense of touch we might imagine feeling the flames which envelop and burn the souls and bodies of the damned. In this regard, we might think of what happened to 35,000+ people burned alive in the fire-bombing raid on Dresden, Germany in 1944. Some spiritual writers try to bring out the meaning of this by pointing out that sinners will be punished especially in the members of their body that they misused in such a way as to bring about their damnation—eyes, taste, touch, mind, memory, imagination, etc.

It is impossible for us in this life to get an adequate idea or image of Hell. Jesus gives us some intimation of it in Luke 16 and Matthew 25. Hell is mortal sin carried out to its ultimate, and sin we can understand only from its effects—in us, in the human race, and in the bloody death on the cross of the only Son of God. The choice is clear: either the Cross or Hell.

Hell means complete desolation, incarceration in self, aloneness, darkness of the soul thrown back upon itself with no help either from other rational creatures or from God. There is no love there, or community or socializing. It is an eternal going around in the cell of self, a purposeless existence—which should have a purpose—stretched out to eternity, that is, no beginning, middle or end—only a perpetual present. Hell, therefore, is a state of absolute abandonment of all that counts in human spiritual existence and a state of rebellion of all things below man against him.

In reflecting on Hell, I should not concentrate much on the damnation of others. The point here is to come to the existential realization that eternal damnation is a real possibility for me personally! I can hope that all men will be saved; I can think well of others; but as I soberly consider Hell I should say with St. Teresa of Avila as I peer into the black, bottomless pit: "That is the Hell into which I can fall!"

Here I can also consider the perilous situation of my human freedom: this Hell can rise out of my heart and soul if I do not love and serve God as I ought. Hell is a state of total frustration of all human desires. And it would have been so easy to avoid it — by corresponding to God's grace, by keeping the Commandments, and by loving God. St. Robert Bellarmine in 1599 dreaded the thought of being made a Cardinal by Pope Clement VIII; he pleaded to be spared but the Pope ordered him under pain of excommunication to stop his pleading, so under obedience he accepted. He did not want the honor because he considered it a danger to his eternal salvation.

Thoughts like these about Hell for the Christian believer are not depressing; they are designed to bring humility into my love of God; I must never forget that I am completely dependent on him and that it is only his love and his grace that stand between me and the eternal pit, and that sin produced Hell.

Thinking seriously about Hell should make us aware of how superficial our culture is. We live in a materialistic, consumer-oriented society that is totally absorbed with money, pleasure and power; it is a culture that does not want us to think about God, moral obligation, death, and eternity in either Heaven or Hell.

Every day we get closer to death and eternity. God made us for himself and he is absolute goodness and beauty. He is our final end, whether we think about it or not. The purpose of reflecting on the reality of Hell is to put some humility in our love for God and the practice of our Catholic religion. Because God is infinite goodness, we should love him for himself because he made us and gave us everything we have except our own sins. God is love and he who abides in love abides in God and God in him. But St. Ignatius of Loyola said that, if we cannot avoid mortal sin because of love for God, we should avoid it because of the fear of Hell. That is a wholesome and healthy fear.

Some people, whether friends or famous media personalities, like to shock us with their use of four-letter words. The most shocking four-letter word of all is "HELL"—especially when you reflect on what it really means as a possible future separated from God for all eternity.

PURGATORY

One of the casualties in the aftermath of Vatican II was the teaching of the Church on the existence of Purgatory and the need to offer Masses and prayers for the souls of relatives and friends who have died.

Today I would like to explain briefly what the Church says about Purgatory: what it is, who goes there, and how long are they detained there.

Purgatory is an exercise of the justice of God. God is infinitely merciful but also infinitely just. The two complement each other. Because of God's infinite goodness and holiness, no one can enter into his presence unless he is totally clean, pure and holy. Jesus himself said that we should be perfect as our heavenly Father is perfect (Matt. 5:48). This means that those who die in the state of sanctifying grace, if they are guilty of any venial sins and if they have not made complete satisfaction for the sins they have committed during their life, must be cleansed and purified before they can be admitted to heaven.

It is important to note, first of all, that the existence of Purgatory is a dogma of the Catholic faith. This means that it is infallibly true that there is a Purgatory, which is a place or condition in which souls of the just are purified of the punishment due to their sins before they are admitted to heaven and the face to face vision of God.

The word "purgation" means to make pure or clean—it comes from two Latin words: "purus" and "agere," that is, make clean. Purgatory is the place or condition in which that takes place. Purgatory has to do with the relation between man and God. God is all-holy and man is a sinner. Sin is an offense against God and is absolutely opposed to him, so no sinner can approach God unless he has been totally cleansed of all sins and the punishment due to sins.

Private revelations to saints tell us that even very holy nuns and monks who have spent years dedicated to prayer and penance, spend time in Purgatory before they can be admitted into the presence of God. This is for minor faults and imperfections. If that is the case with Carmelite nuns and Carthusian monks, then how foolish it is for us to think that we or a pious relative goes directly to heaven after death. A practical consequence of the truth about Purgatory is that we should always offer Masses and prayers for loved ones who die to help them get to heaven as soon as possible.

We are not certain about the nature of the punishment or purgation that takes place in Purgatory, since we are dealing with souls separated from their body. In Scripture and in the Fathers it is referred to as "fire" or something like fire. The Church does not teach that it is a "physical fire," even though many preachers, theologians and catechisms speak of "the fires of Purgatory." The official declarations of the Councils speak only of "purifying punishments," not of purifying fire. But whatever it is, it is very painful. St. Thomas Aquinas says that one hour in purgatory involves more suffering than many years of intense suffering on earth.

Also, suffering in Purgatory is not the same for all, since the sinfulness of individuals is different. It is like debtors in this life— some have debts of a few dollars, while others owe millions of dollars to their creditors. The length of time in Purgatory depends on the size of the debt to be paid and the seriousness of the sins one has committed.

Through the constant practice and belief of the Church we know that the sufferings of the souls in Purgatory can be alleviated by the Masses, prayers and penances of faithful Christians on earth. This truth is intimately related to the communion of saints and the Mystical body of Christ. We all form one Church in different stages. The souls in Purgatory cannot merit, which means that they cannot do anything by themselves to shorten their stay in Purgatory, but we can help them by our prayers and gaining indulgences for them. This is another reason why we should constantly pray for the souls in Purgatory.

Unlike hell where there is no hope, Purgatory in not a place of despair. In the midst of the suffering there is great joy because the souls in Purgatory know that they are saved and that, eventually, they will be admitted to the eternal bliss of heaven. That being the case, they willingly suffer for their sins while they wait to be released.

We can help the souls in Purgatory by gaining INDULGENCES for them. An indulgence is the remission of the punishment due to sins because of the infinite merits of Jesus Christ, and the abundant merits of the Blessed Virgin Mary and all the saints. It is like a huge bank filled with treasures and administered by the Church. There are two types of indulgences: partial and plenary: A partial indulgence means just that—a part of their debt is paid, but not all of it, by a Catholic who performs the good work to which an indulgence is attached, such as saying a Rosary before the Blessed Sacrament or making the Stations of the Cross in church.

A plenary indulgence means the full remission of the punishment of a soul in Purgatory. So if uncle Joe dies on Saturday and is sentenced to Purgatory for many years, and on Sunday I gain a plenary indulgence for him, this means that he is released immediately from Purgatory and goes straight to heaven. Catholics who know their faith put a high value on plenary indulgences.

There are five conditions that must be fulfilled in order to gain a plenary indulgence: 1) perform a certain work, such as saying a Rosary before the Blessed Sacrament or spending a half hour reading the Bible; 2) have the intention of gaining the indulgence; 3) receive Holy Communion on that day; 4) go to confession eight days before or eight days after the good work is done; 5) not be attached to any sin, mortal or venial.

We should be generous in gaining and offering up indulgences for the souls in Purgatory. It helps them get to heaven and it also helps us: we now have a friend in heaven who will be praying for us and seeking God's grace for us so that we will grow in holiness and save our soul.

St. Teresa of Avila said that she knew of only three persons who went straight to heaven without having to go to Purgatory: St. Peter of Alcantara, a friar, and a holy Dominican priest. Our Lady of Fatima told the children that a girl of 17 that they knew would be in Purgatory until the end of the world! That is truly frightening.

Years ago a woman wrote to me and told me that her mother was a very holy woman and the priest, at her funeral Mass, said she was in heaven. So the daughter did not offer any prayers or Masses for her mother, thinking she was in heaven. Then one day she read a pamphlet on Purgatory and realized that her mother might be in Purgatory and she had done nothing in fourteen years to help her. She said she immediately started to offer prayers and Masses for her mother.

A member of a Secular Institute, who was sick and dying, wrote to me that it was hard for her to be good when she was sick. She was afraid that she might commit a sin of anger and die in that state. So she asked me to pray that she would die soon in the state of grace and go to Purgatory. "If I get to Purgatory," she wrote, "then I am sure of getting to heaven." That is a very Catholic sentiment.

In our prayers and sufferings, we should not forget to offer them to God for the souls of our loved ones, relatives and friends, seeking indulgences for them so that their stay in Purgatory will be shortened as much as possible. Private revelations tell us that some souls may have to spend a long time in purgatory, but can be released early through the prayers and sacrifices of the faithful on earth. If we help them to get to heaven then we will have friends there to pray for us when we need help and can no longer help ourselves. Amen.

SIN

Man desires perfect happiness which consists in unlimited goodness and beauty. That is what God is, so man's perfect happiness consists in a loving union with God. Most people do not seem to know that, but when they seek happiness in creatures and pleasure, none of which can ever make them truly happy, what they are really searching for is God.

We know from divine revelation that God created man for eternal happiness: "God so loved the world that he sent his only-begotten Son into the world that whose who believe in him might not perish, but have life everlasting" (John 3:16). In order to achieve eternal happiness and union with God, man must live according to reason and divine revelation which is contained in the Bible and the teaching of the Church.

Man is the only being on earth who has freedom of choice. Everything else achieves its end necessarily according to the laws of nature. We do not praise or blame rocks, trees and animals for doing what their nature tells them to do. Man is free to choose his end or to reject it. So only man is worthy of praise or blame, according to how he uses his freedom. Rejecting the end for which he is created is what we mean by sin. Sin in all its forms is to choose and prefer a creature in place of the Creator. Pride, putting oneself in the place of God, is involved in all sins.

St. Augustine said that sin is any word, deed or thought contrary to the law of God. The Old Testament uses several words for what we mean by sin. In the English translation most of the Hebrew words are translated with the word "sin." But there are shades of difference in meaning: One word means "missing the mark" or "going the wrong way." Another word means "iniquity, guilt." A third one means "to rebel or to transgress against." A fourth one means "bad or evil." All four are often translated into English as "sin."

Man is bound by the law of nature or natural law which tells him in his conscience to do good and avoid evil. In the practical order this comes down to doing what is reasonable by respecting the rights of others. All this is basically summarized in the Ten Commandments, which can be expressed by love of God and love of neighbor as oneself. A simple definition of sin is that it is aversion from God and conversion towards creatures. It means putting creatures in the place of God—preferring creatures to God.

Sin is rooted in the human free will. It is good for man to follow God's law; it is evil for him to rebel against that law and to put a creature in the place of God, such as sex, money, honor, political power, food and drink.

There are both internal causes of sin and external causes. The internal causes are ignorance, passion from the senses, and malice because of a distorted will. The external causes of sin are the devil and the world. There is also Original Sin which we inherit from Adam. Because of Adam's sin we have concupiscence which is a tendency towards rebellion against God, and love of self to the point of violating the rights of others.

Mortal Sin separates man from God. In the real order this means that man loses sanctifying grace which is the life of God and the life of the soul. A person who dies in the state of mortal sin will go directly to hell and will be separated from God forever. St. Paul gives a list of some mortal sins in Galatians 5:19–21: "Now the works of the flesh are plain: immorality, impurity, licentiousness, idolatry, sorcery, enmity, strife, jealousy, anger, selfishness, dissension, party spirit, envy, drunkenness, carousing and the like. I warn you, as I warned you before, that those who do such things shall not inherit the kingdom of God."

There are two aspects of sin: guilt and punishment. There is guilt because of the offense against God. The guilt of sin can be removed by repentance and asking God for forgiveness, especially in the Sacrament of Penance, which he will always grant if the person is sincere and truly repentant. But there is also punishment associated with sin. The Church calls that "the temporal punishment due to sin." This can be taken away by penance in this life (prayer, fasting and almsgiving), or by suffering in purgatory after one dies in the state of grace.

Catholic theologians distinguish two kinds of sin: mortal sin and venial sin. Mortal sin is a serious offense against God. As a result, the sinner loses sanctifying grace which makes one a child of God and heir of heaven. He loses the friendship of God. If one dies in this state, he goes directly to hell forever. In order to commit a mortal sin, there must be <u>serious matter</u> (murder, adultery, blasphemy, etc.), <u>sufficient reflection</u> of what one is doing, that is, one must know that it is evil and forbidden by God, and <u>full consent of the will</u>. If one of these is lacking, it will be a venial sin.

Venial sin is any offense against God which is less than a mortal sin, such as telling a lie of convenience, speaking uncharitably of others, impatience, eating too much, gossiping, avoiding one's duties, and so forth. Venial sins can be either deliberate or indeliberate. In any event, they lessen one's love of God and, if deliberate, can lead one gradually into mortal sin. Venial sins do not destroy sanctifying grace, but they diminish it. They can be removed by repentance and confession, but if one dies with venial sins on his soul, he will have to make restitution for them by the sufferings of purgatory. Such a person is unclean and is not ready to be admitted into heaven and the face to face vision of God.

The cause of the sorry plight of human beings, all of them, is the reality of SIN—the sin of Adam and the personal sins of our ancestors and of each person. Sin is the reason for suffering in all its forms—disease, cancer, murder, theft, war and so forth—and death for everyone. In 1968 Fr. William G. Heidt, O.S.B., published a booklet in the series of Old Testament Reading Guides (The Liturgical Press, #30) in which he argued that sin is the major theme of the Old Testament. My comments here are based on his research.

The primary role of sin in the history of mankind is clearly expressed in the words of consecration of the wine at Mass: THIS IS THE CUP OF MY BLOOD, THE BLOOD OF THE NEW AND EVERLASTING COVENANT... THIS BLOOD WILL BE SHED FOR YOU AND FOR MANY SO THAT <u>SINS</u> MAY BE FORGIVEN.

The New Testament says many times that the reason for the Incarnation of God was and is to save men from their sins. The

Messiah promised in the Old Testament is Jesus and the name "Jesus" means "savior." Savior from what? Savior from sin and the consequences of sin. In the very first chapter of the New Testament, the angel said to Joseph: "Joseph, son of David, do not fear to take Mary as your wife.... she will bear a son, and you shall call his name Jesus, for he will save his people from their sins" (Matt. 1:21).

Here are more quotes from the New Testament which say the same thing: "This saying is true and worthy of full acceptance, that Christ Jesus came into the world in order to save sinners" (1 Tim. 1:15). "God sent his Son in order to be the expiation of our sins" (1 John 4:10). "God shows his love for us in that while we were yet sinners Christ died for us" (Rom. 5:8).

So the purpose of the Incarnation, the reason why God became man in Jesus Christ is, to save man from sin. According to Fr. Heidt, the primary purpose of the Bible is not to reveal the love of God for man. His motive is love, but the purpose or goal is to save mankind from sin (*ibid.*, pp. 4–5). This theme of liberation from sin runs all through the Old Testament—in the Torah, in the prophets, in the history books and in the wisdom books. It is especially prominent in Genesis, Exodus, Leviticus, Numbers, Deuteronomy; it is evident in the book of Judges and in the books of Kings; it is evident in the Psalms, especially Ps. 51; it is evident also in the wisdom books like Job, Ecclesiastes, Sirach and Wisdom. If you were to remove the theme of sin from the Bible—its cause, its effects and its cure—there would not be much left.

In the New Testament John the Baptist appears at the Jordan preaching repentance for sins and baptizing for the remission of sins. When Jesus appears, John proclaims to his audience: 'Behold the Lamb of God, behold him who takes away the sins of the world" (John 1:29). Jesus' first words in Mark's Gospel are: "The time is fulfilled, and the kingdom of God has come hear; repent, and believe in the good news" (Mark 1:15). In the first Christian sermon on Pentecost Sunday, St. Peter told the crowd in Jerusalem: "Repent, and be baptized every one of you in the name of Jesus

Christ so that your sins may be forgiven" (Acts 2:38). So repentance for sin is a key factor in all Christian preaching.

As Catholics we should rejoice that we have the Sacrament of Penance through which the grace of Christ is communicated to us for the forgiveness of all sins, provided that one is truly repentant and has purpose of amendment.

Sorrow for sin, asking for forgiveness of sins, and asking for protection against sin and evil, are very frequent ideas contained in the prayers of the Church as found in the Entrance Rite of the traditional Mass and also in the Collect, Secret and Post-communion of Sunday and weekday Masses.

In the Confiteor the priest prays (and also the altar boys): "I confess to almighty God... that I have sinned exceedingly in thought, word and deed." Immediately after the Confiteor the priest prays: "May Almighty God have mercy upon you, forgive you your sins, and bring you to life everlasting." After the Amen of the altar boys he then prays: "May the Almighty and merciful God grant us pardon, absolution, and remission of our sins."

After those prayers, as the priest ascends the altar he prays: "Take away from us our iniquities, we entreat Thee, O Lord, that with pure minds we may worthily enter into the Holy of Holies. Through Christ our Lord. Amen." Then he adds: "We beseech Thee, O Lord, by the merits of Thy Saints, whose relics are here, and of all the Saints, that Thou wilt deign to pardon me all my sins. Amen."

Next, after the Introit prayer the priest begs God for mercy nine times with the Kyrie Eleison. With these prayers we see clearly that the Church is very serious about asking God for pardon of our sins before beginning the Canon of the Mass and the consecration of bread and wine into the Body and Blood of Christ. Sorrow for sin and seeking forgiveness of sin are common themes that occur in many of the prayers of the Mass. Following are a few examples of the sin-awareness contained in many of the prayers in the Mass:

a. [First Sunday of Advent, Collect]: "Stir up Thy power, we beseech Thee, O Lord, and come: that from the threatening dangers of our sins, by Thy protection we may deserve to be rescued, and be saved by Thy deliverance."

b. [Third Sunday of Advent, Post-communion]: "We implore Thy mercy, O Lord, that these divine mysteries, by atoning for our sins, may prepare us for the coming festival."

c. [Saturday in Ember Week of Advent, Collect]: "Grant, we beseech Thee, almighty God, that we who are oppressed by the former servitude under the yoke of sin, may be delivered by the new birth of Thine only-begotten Son, for which we long."

d. [Christmas, Third Mass, Collect]: "Grant, we beseech Thee, almighty God, that the new birth in the flesh of Thine only-begotten Son may set us free, whom the old bondage doth hold under the yoke of sin." [Secret]: "The gifts we offer, do Thou, O Lord, sanctify by the new birth of Thine only-begotten Son: and cleanse us from the stains of our sins."

e. [January 1, Post-communion]: "May this communion, O Lord, cleanse us from all sin: and by the intercession of the Blessed Virgin Mary, Mother of God, make us partakers of the heavenly remedy."

f. [Second Sunday after Epiphany, Secret]: "Sanctify, O Lord, the gifts which we offer, and cleanse us from the stains of our sins."

g. [Septuagesima Sunday, Collect]: "Graciously hear, we beseech Thee, O Lord, the prayers of Thy people, that we who are justly afflicted for our sins, may be mercifully delivered by thy goodness, for the glory of Thy name."

h. [Third Sunday of Lent, Secret]: "May this offering, we beseech Thee, O Lord, cleanse away our sins, sanctifying

Thy servants in both soul and body for the celebration of this sacrifice."

i. [Feast of the Sacred Heart of Jesus, Collect]: "O God, who in the Heart of Thy Son, wounded by our sins, dost mercifully vouchsafe to bestow upon us the infinite wealth of Thy love; grant, we beseech Thee, that revering it with meet devotion, we may fulfill our duty of worthy reparation."

These few liturgical prayers will give you some idea of the Church's awareness of the importance of sin, sorrow for sin and forgiveness of sin in the life of each person. The Church begs God often to forgive the sins of the faithful and to grant them the grace to resist and overcome sin.

Since sin is a thought, word or action contrary to reason on the natural level and contrary to the divine law on the supernatural level, the remedy of sin is always to act reasonably, to adhere to the will of God, to obey God. The main remedy of sin is faith in Jesus Christ, Baptism and so becoming a member of his Church. That gives one access to all the sacraments, especially the Mass, Holy Communion and the Sacrament of Penance for the forgiveness of sins.

Sins are committed because of the influence of the world, the flesh and the devil. The Christian, fortified with the sacraments of the Church and sanctifying grace, is given from and through Christ the spiritual power to resist temptation and to overcome it. A key factor in the battle against sin is daily prayer. St. Paul says that the Christian should pray always. Those who pray always are the most successful in resisting temptation and in avoiding sin. Especially helpful is daily attendance at Mass and regular confession.

It should be obvious from the above that sin—rebellion against God who is the source of being, life and goodness—is the greatest evil in the world. If everyone obeyed the Ten Commandments and practiced love of God and neighbor, there would be a paradise on earth. There would be no idolatry, no lying, no theft, no murder, no adultery and other sexual sins, no envy, no jealousy. There would be no need for armies and huge police forces, no need for missiles and bombers. We can all make this a better world first of all by avoiding all deliberate sins in our own personal life and by putting into practice the commandment of love preached by Jesus: love God above all things and our neighbor as our self. If everyone did that, we would live in a world at peace.

ETERNITY

In the past few weeks I have spoken to you about heaven and hell. An essential aspect of these two possible futures for all human beings is their participation in the eternity of God. Those who go to heaven share in eternal life; those who go to hell are subjected to eternal punishment. Today I want to speak to you about eternity and what the Church means by eternal life.

In ordinary language we sometimes speak about things being "forever." That means without end. Popular love songs often use words like, "I will love you forever and forever." We have daily experience of time—minutes, hours, days, weeks, months and years. When we say that something will last "forever," we mean that it will not have an end. That touches on what the Bible means by "eternal life" and "everlasting life." Time is a measure of motion of before and after; the idea of eternity is of permanent existence, a permanent now, with no before or after.

Time and eternity both refer to some kind of duration in existence. Time has to do with motion, constant change, a measure of before and after. Eternity is also duration in being, but it is a permanent now, with no before and after, with no beginning and no end. The best definition of eternity is that it is "the simultaneously-whole and perfect possession of interminable life" (Boethius). Eternity is life without end, all at once with permanent possession. No change is possible, so it cannot be lost and also it cannot be added to.

In the full sense, only God is eternal because only he is immutable and has no beginning and no end. Spiritual creatures, like angels and the human soul, are naturally immortal. They have a beginning, since they were created, but they have no end. So that is what we mean by eternal life—it is permanent life, a constant perpetual now, with no end. Usually we are aware of the passage of time—morning, noon and evening. Sometimes, however, when we are very happy and enjoying the company of those we love, we can pass a few hours without being aware of the passage of time. When we are happy like that, we say that "time flies." Eternal life is something like that.

Eternity, eternal life and eternal death are mentioned many times in the Bible. It occurs in the Psalms in the Old Testament, but especially in the New Testament. In the Gospels our Lord mentions eternal life many times, and he mentions hell and eternal damnation over thirty times. Let me quote a few texts from the Bible to show you what I mean:

a. Ps. 90:4, "In your sight a thousand years are as the passing of one day or as a watch in the night."

b. Ps. 102:27, "But you are the same and your years have no end."

c. Jesus says in John 17:3, "This is eternal life: to know you the only true God, and Jesus Christ whom you have sent."

d. John 3:16, "God so loved the world that he gave his only Son, that everyone who has faith in him may not perish but have eternal life."

e. Peter said to Jesus after his sermon on the Bread of Life: "Lord, to whom shall we go? Your words are words of eternal life" (John 6:68).

f. In the parable of the sheep and goats in Matthew 25, the king says at the conclusion regarding the good and the bad, "And they will go away to eternal punishment, but the righteous will enter eternal life" (Matt. 25:46).

g. We noted that "lack of succession" is essential to eternity. This idea is found in Jesus' remarkable words. "I tell you most solemnly, before Abraham ever was, I AM" (John 8:58).

That is just a sampling of the many references to eternity in the Bible. The Church teaches us that God is eternal. We also find it in the liturgy in the various creeds. In the Apostles' Creed we pray: "I believe in the resurrection of the body and life everlasting." At Mass in the Nicene Creed we say, "I believe... in the life of the world to come."

It is a sobering thought to think that eternity is my destiny—it is a reality I cannot escape. God made me immortal, which means that I have an eternal destiny of either heaven or hell. There is no other alternative, such as annihilation. I am destined for either eternal happiness or eternal misery. This was beautifully and effectively captured by the great Italian poet, Dante, in his *Divine Comedy,* written in the 14th century.

Since we live in a secular and materialistic culture, spiritual realities are ignored, especially revealed truths about eternity, the devil and hell. The common assumption in our culture now, either explicit or implicit, is that man's life totally ends with death. And those who do believe in the future life seem to assume that everyone goes to heaven. Most people seem to believe in heaven, but very few believe in hell.

As a Catholic, I should take the teaching of the Church about eternity very seriously. Life is not a game; it is serious business, especially when you realize that you will live forever— either happily or miserably. Since I am a limited creature, I had my beginning in my mother's womb when God created me. I had a beginning, but there is no end to my life. Death of the body, which comes to all of us, means entrance of my soul, my person, into eternity with God. At Jesus' Second Coming at the end of the world, I will rise from the dead to live forever—either in heaven or in hell. St. Paul tells us that now is the time of salvation; now is the time to grow in the knowledge and love of God. Now is the time to work out my salvation in fear and trembling (see Phil 2:12).

In order to reach heaven and to gain eternal life I must live the way God designed me to live. That means receiving the Sacraments of the Church, praying every day, self-restraint and controlling evil desires, trying to live according to God's law, and practicing love of God and love of neighbor. Basically, it means seeking God's will in all things and living my life according to his rules, not the rule of any modern philosophy or ideology.

Thoughts about eternity are very sobering. My life now on this earth, at this time and in this century, is a preparation for my eternal life. God made me free and he will not force me to live according to his rules. He gives most of us 70 or 80 years to work out our salvation. He invites me to do so, and he sends me his grace to help me, but he will not force me. He respects my freedom. So my eternal future is in my hands.

Life is a great adventure—the greatest of all adventures. This reflection on eternity—eternal life or eternal misery—is meant to help you put order into your life and to motivate you to accept God's grace and to live the way he wants you to live so that you can attain eternal, everlasting happiness.

THE SEVEN GIFTS OF THE HOLY SPIRIT: SAILS OF THE SOUL

The spirit of the Lord shall rest on him, the spirit of wisdom and understanding, the spirit of counsel and might, the spirit of knowledge and the fear of the Lord.

(Isaiah 11:2)

In this series of sermons we have reflected on the infused theological and moral virtues. Today I want to speak to you about the Seven Gifts of the Holy Spirit which are given to us at our Baptism along with sanctifying grace. Surely you have heard them mentioned at some time in a catechism class, in your reading, or in a sermon.

You probably have never heard a complete sermon on the Gifts of the Holy Spirit. They are: wisdom, understanding, knowledge, counsel, fortitude, piety, and fear of the Lord. I will not try to explain each one in detail today—it would take too long. Rather, I will explain what they are as group, what they do for us, and their importance in our life of faith to help us save our souls and reach heaven.

The Gifts are supernatural principles or permanent dispositions given by God to our spiritual faculties of intellect and will or appetite. The virtues are principles of operation, like faith, hope and charity. They are active. The Gifts are more passive and enable us to receive help from the Holy Spirit to practice virtue and lead a good Christian life; they make it possible for us to recognize and follow inspirations from the Holy Spirit.

St. Thomas compares the Gifts to the sails of a boat and the virtues to the oars of a boat. Let us imagine a couple sailing in a small boat that also has oars. If there is no wind and they want to return to the port, they have to row with the oars; the virtues are like that. If the wind fills the sails, then they return to port easily without having to row; St. Thomas likens the sails to the Gifts—just as the sails catch the wind and move the boat, so the

Gifts catch or receive impulses from the Holy Spirit which perfect the acts of virtue and help us to grow in love of God and holiness of life. In this regard St. Thomas says (I-II, 68, a. 2): "The gifts are perfections of man, whereby he is disposed so as to be amenable to the promptings of God."

Baptism is like a new birth in which we become "a new creature" according to St. Paul. Our new spiritual organism is composed of divine grace, the theological and moral virtues, and the Seven Gifts of the Holy Spirit. You might say that it is a "complete package." As we grow to maturity physically, we also grow, or should grow, spiritually. So as we increase in grace and the love of God, by a Christian life of prayer and the Sacraments, we also grow in all the virtues and the Gifts of the Holy Spirit. The person who tragically falls into mortal sin loses all of that, with the exception of faith and hope, which are not lost unless one sins directly against them by apostasy or despair.

In the Bible, and especially in the New Testament, the Holy Spirit is called "the Gift of God." St. Peter said in his Pentecost sermon (Acts 2:14–42): "Repent and be baptized every one of you in the name of Jesus Christ for the forgiveness of your sins; and you shall receive the gift of the Holy Spirit" (v. 38) (see also 10:45 for the same).

The Holy Spirit with his Gifts is given to us to help us grow in the knowledge and love of God. The Gifts help us to resist temptation, avoid mortal sin, and .practice virtue. In one of his articles, St. Thomas asks whether or not the Gifts will remain with us in heaven. He says that they will remain with us and will be perfectly operative because we will be totally open to receiving God's influence on us (see I-II, 68, a.6).

The Gifts modify or influence or dispose or perfect our higher faculties of intellect and will/appetite. The first four—wisdom, understanding, knowledge and counsel—pertain to knowledge, so they influence our thinking and judging about what is right and what is wrong in daily living. The last three—fortitude, piety and fear of the Lord—pertain to seeking the good and so they influence our will, especially in controlling anger, overindulgence in food or drink, and regulating the sexual drive so that we lead a chaste life.

Here I would like to say just a brief word about each of the Seven Gifts:

a. The Gift of Wisdom helps us to judge rightly concerning God and divine things through their ultimate and highest causes.

b. The Gift of Understanding helps the human mind to penetrate into the deeper meaning of revealed truths, such as the Trinity & Incarnation.

c. The Gift of Knowledge helps the human intellect to judge rightly concerning created things and how they are related to eternal life and Christian perfection.

d. The Gift of Counsel helps the human mind to judge rightly in particular events what ought to be done in view of the supernatural ultimate end of human life.

e. The Gift of Fortitude strengthens the will for the practice of virtue, with invincible confidence of overcoming any dangers or difficulties that may arise.

f. The Gift of Piety arouses in the will a filial love for God as Father, and a sentiment of love for all as our brothers and sisters and children of the same heavenly Father.

g. The gift of Fear of the Lord perfects the virtue of hope by motivating the individual to avoid sin out of reverential fear of God. It also assists the virtue of temperance by helping to moderate emotions of anger, gluttony and lust.

Because of sin, concupiscence and human weakness, we need all the help we can get in order to save our souls and to finally reach heaven. Faith, hope and charity, grace, prayer and the Sacraments are essential to remain faithful to Christ and live a good, Christian life. God's help is always available; the Holy Spirit has been given to us in Baptism, as I said above. By his Gifts, he illumines our mind and inspires our will so we can think, judge and act correctly and morally.

As we grow in virtue, grace and the love of God, the Gifts grow silently in us and gradually make us more attentive and attuned to hear the Word of God and to be led by the Holy Spirit to the final Kingdom of God for which God made us and to which he is calling us. Now that you know something about the Seven Gifts of the Holy Spirit, today you should thank him for them, and ask for the grace always to respond favorably to his illuminations and inspirations so that you may grow in the knowledge and love of God, since that is the ultimate purpose of your life and the reason why God created you in the first place. Amen.

THE TWELVE FRUITS OF THE HOLY SPIRIT

We have already considered the virtues and the gifts of the Holy Spirit which are principles of good actions. Today I would like to speak to you about the "fruits of the Holy Spirit." Every year in the liturgy we read the passage from St. Paul's Letter to the Galatians about the works of the flesh and the fruits of the Holy Spirit. There he lists the twelve fruits of the Holy Spirit: "But the harvest of the Spirit is love, joy, peace, patience, kindness, goodness, fidelity, gentleness, self-control, modesty, continence and chastity. Against such things there is no law" (Gal. 5:22–23). As in the case of the gifts of the Holy Spirit, surely you have heard of these "fruits" in catechism class, and also have heard them read at Mass once a year, but you probably have never had them explained to you. What I propose to do today is to tell you in simple language what the Church and St. Thomas say about these twelve fruits.

The fruits of the Holy Spirit are acts of virtue and acts that flow from the Seven Gifts of the Holy Spirit. When we use the word "fruit" here we are using metaphorical language. The reason for the existence of fruit trees—apples, oranges, pears, plums, and so forth—is to produce fruit to nourish men and animals. The final product of the tree is the fruit which is also characterized by a certain sweetness.

When the word "fruit" is applied to the acts of human beings, it refers to the good actions of the human person—acts of love, joy, kindness, gentleness, patience, modesty and chastity. We know what a thing is from what it does; we can only know what powers a tree or animal has when we see what they do. Our Lord said in this regard, "By their fruits you shall know them" (Matt. 12:33), that is to say, men are known by their works. Therefore, since such acts are like the products of a tree, they are called his "fruits."

St. Paul lists twelve of them. The first four have to do with the individual person himself –love, joy, peace, patience; the others have to do with other persons, things, or one's own passions: kindness, goodness, fidelity, gentleness (or meekness), self-control, modesty, continence and chastity. These fruits of the Spirit are virtuous acts that we are able to perform because of the assistance of the Holy Spirit in us. Fruits, like oranges, apples and pears, are sweet, tasty and delightful. These virtuous acts are called "fruits" precisely because of the spiritual delight they produce. You can see the working of these fruits in the face and smile and personal demeanor of cloistered Carmelite nuns who lead a very penitential life and are totally dedicated to the service of God. They radiate happiness because they are filled with the Holy Spirit and are experiencing the delights of his fruits—especially love, joy and peace.

St. Thomas Aquinas said: "Every virtuous act which man performs with pleasure is a fruit." So the fruits are not habits or powers, but acts. They are not the same thing as virtues and gifts, because they are their effects. They are called "fruits" because they are acts which are performed with ease and pleasure, in a way similar to the pleasure one gets from eating apples and oranges.

At our Baptism we receive the Holy Spirit. St. Paul says in Romans 5:5: "God's love has been poured into our hearts through the Holy Spirit that has been given to us." The Holy Spirit abides in us, along with the Father and the Son, as Jesus says in John 14:23: "If you love me, you will keep my word, and my Father will love you and we will come to you and abide with you." Again in John 14:26: "But the advocate, the Holy Spirit whom the Father will send in my name, will teach you everything and remind you of all that I have told you."

Everyone in the state of grace has the Holy Spirit residing within him. The more we follow his inspirations and illuminations, and the more we strive to practice love of God and neighbor in all areas of our life, the happier we will be and the more we will experience the joy of the fruits of the Holy Spirit. So the good deeds we perform under the influence of the Holy Spirit are called his "fruits."

In Galatians 5:16–26 St. Paul contrasts the "works of the flesh" with the fruits of the Holy Spirit. Here is what he says: "Live by the Spirit, I say, and do not gratify the desires of the flesh.

For what the flesh desires is opposed to the Spirit, and what the Spirit desires is opposed to the flesh; for these are opposed to each other, to prevent you from doing what you want. But if you are led by the Spirit, you are not subject to the law. Now the works of the flesh are obvious: fornication, impurity, licentiousness, idolatry, sorcery, enmities, strife, jealousy, anger, quarrels, dissensions, factions, envy, drunkenness, carousing, and things like these. I am warning you, as I warned you before: those who do such things will not inherit the kingdom of God" (Gal. 5:16–21).

Those who are not led by the Spirit are sinners who rebel against God. Their works are evil: they shame their own bodies; they rebel against God; they injure others in various ways and come into conflict with them. These are the "works of the flesh" which are contrary to reason and are forbidden by the Ten Commandments. How different they are from the "fruits of the Spirit" that he lists in the following verses which we have already considered. After listing the fruits of the Spirit, St. Paul goes on to say, "Against such things there is no law," that is, it is not necessary to have a law regarding the fruits or acts of the virtues and the gifts of the Holy Spirit because they are always good. St. Paul goes on to say in verses 24 and 25: "And those who belong to Christ Jesus have crucified the flesh with its passions and desires. If we live by the Spirit, let us also be guided by the Spirit."

Much more could be said about the fruits of the Holy Spirit, but that will have to do for now. Every person seeks happiness in whatever he does—work, play, study, recreation, eating, drinking, sleeping, visiting with others. The secret in life is to find out what true happiness is and to strive to live accordingly. True happiness is not to be found in inordinate attachment to alcohol, food, sex, riches, political power, fame or any created thing. As the saints discovered, happiness is found in doing the will of God in all things. If we strive to do that each day, with the help of prayer and the Sacraments of the Church, we will surely experience and enjoy the fruits of the Holy Spirit.

OUR FATHER

Our Father who art in heaven

Jesus was a man of prayer. Often he spent the whole night in prayer. His disciples, of course, often saw him praying. On one occasion they said to him, "Lord, teach us to pray, as John taught his disciples" (Luke 11:1). In reply Jesus taught them the "Our Father" which is the most common Christian prayer.

The "Our Father" is often referred to as "the Lord's Prayer" because it was given to us by the Lord Jesus. Tertullian said that it is truly the summary of the whole Gospel. St. Thomas Aquinas said: "The Lord's prayer is the most perfect of prayers.... In it we ask, not only for all the things we can rightly desire, but also in the sequence that they should be desired. This prayer not only teaches us to ask for things, but also in what order we should desire them" (S.Th. II-II, 83, 9). The Lord's Prayer is at the center of the Scriptures; it is also the center of the famous Sermon on the Mount in Matthew 5 to 7.

In all the liturgical traditions of East and West the Lord's Prayer is an integral part of the Divine Office. In the three sacraments of Christian initiation—Baptism, Confirmation and Eucharist—it has a special place. At every Mass, before receiving Holy Communion, the Church directs us to pray "audemus dicere," we make bold to say, "Our Father...."

The prayer consists of an initial invocation of God as "Our Father who art in heaven," then there are seven petitions—three that concern the majesty of God and four that refer to our corporal and spiritual needs in order to lead good Christian lives that will get us finally to heaven. Here I will offer a brief explanation of the opening invocation of the Lord's Prayer.

I. "Father"

To be a father means to be the principle or source of some other being.

As such it implies a relation to a child. So when we call God our Father, it means that he is the principle or source of our being. The notion of "father" is applied to God in the primary sense that the Father is the eternal principle of the Son. This means that the idea of "father" applies to him essentially from all eternity before God created the heavens and the earth. In an analogous or secondary sense, he is our father because he created us from nothing, he provides for us by keeping us in existence, and he redeemed us by sending his Son into the world as our Savior. Jesus Christ, the Second Person of the Blessed Trinity, is the natural Son of God; we are sons of God only as his adopted children through the grace of Jesus Christ. So our relation to the heavenly Father is not the same as that of Jesus to his Father. Thus, Jesus never prays "Our Father, "but always "My Father," because he was eternally generated from the substance of the Father.

Since God created man in his own image, it is with good reason that, in view of the unique privilege with which he has honored man, the Bible calls God the Father of all men; not only of the faithful, but also of the unbelieving.

By his providence God cares for us and keeps order in the world. By a special governing care and providence over our interests God displays a paternal love for us. He cares for us by assigning a Guardian Angel to each one of us to help us on our way to heaven. This is explained beautifully in the book of Tobit where we read that the angel Raphael guided Tobias and brought him back home safe and sound; he saved him from being devoured by an enormous fish; he expelled the demon; he taught the young man the true and legitimate notion and use of matrimony; and finally he restored to the elder Tobias the use of his sight.

To the Israelites who had complained that God had abandoned them, Isaiah answered: "Can a woman forget her infant, so as not to have pity on the son of her womb? And if she should forget, yet I will not forget thee. Behold, I have engraved thee in the palms of my hands" (Isa. 49:14ff).

God is also called Father because he has granted us redemption. Far above the gifts of creation and providence shines the work of redemption, so much so that our bountiful God and Father has crowned his infinite goodness towards us by granting us this third and supernatural favor. Thus, Baptism is the sacrament of regeneration through water and the word which makes us children of God. By reason of our redemption we have received the Holy Spirit and the grace of God. Because of this we are the adopted children of God, as St. Paul says: "For you did not receive the spirit of slavery to fall back into fear, but you have received the spirit of sonship. When we cry, 'Abba! Father!' it is the Spirit himself bearing witness with our spirit that we are children of God" (Rom. 8:15–16).

The Father's love for us is so great that we can never thank him adequately. Because of his goodness to us, we owe him adoration, thanks and the obedience of faith that St. Paul speaks about in his letter to the Romans.

II. "Our"

When we pray to God as "our" Father we are, of course, not asserting any kind of ownership. Since we are all his adopted children, the possessive pronoun means that we form a community of believers, that we are all brothers and sisters in Christ. Jesus said to his disciples, "You are all brethren... for you have one Father who is in heaven" (Matt. 23:8–9).

Another result of this adoption is that we are also brothers of Jesus Christ, our Redeemer. Since Jesus is truly a man, he is one of us and so he is our brother. After his resurrection he said to the women, "Go and tell my brethren to go to Galilee, and there they will see me" (Matt. 28:10).

Christians come from all walks in life—rich and poor, male and female, learned and illiterate, young and old—but all are members of Christ's body and so related to each other through possession of the same divine life and the same Holy Spirit. So we are all brothers in the Lord. This is shown in a special way by mutual love and charity.

III. "Who art in heaven"

When we say that the Father is in heaven we mean that he transcends all time and place; he is not contained in any place, but he contains all the universe and keeps it in existence. His being is spiritual and eternal, not material and temporal like everything in the universe. Because God keeps all things in existence, he is everywhere. He is in all places, especially in the soul of man. For believers who are in the state of sanctifying grace he is present in a new and special way, as St. Paul says, "Don't you know that you are the temple of God?"

Even though God is everywhere, Scripture often says that he is in heaven. The reason is that the heavens which we see above our heads are the noblest part of the world, surpass all other bodies in power, grandeur and beauty, and are endowed with a fixed and regular motion.

In order to lift up the minds of men to contemplate his infinite power and majesty, which are so visible in the work of the heavens, God declares in the Bible that heaven is his dwelling place. At the same time he also says that he is everywhere intimately present by his essence and power.

In order to find true happiness we must seek the things that are eternal and lasting. I would like to conclude with the words of St. Paul in Colossians 3:1, "If then you have been raised with Christ, seek the things that are above, where Christ is, seated at the right hand of God. Set your minds on things that are above, not on things that are on earth."

OUR FATHER 1 – THY NAME

Hallowed be thy name

After placing ourselves in the presence of God the Father, we direct seven petitions to him. The first three concern the glory and majesty of God; the next four concern our corporal and spiritual needs. Today we will reflect on the first petition, "hallowed be thy name."

"Hallowed" is an old English word that means to be sanctified or to be made holy. God is holiness itself and the essence of all holiness. "Name" here stands for the Person of the Father. So the meaning is: we pray that God himself may be recognized as holy by all peoples, that they will glorify him and praise him for his goodness and his infinite majesty. In this regard St. Paul says that we should be "holy and blameless before him in love" (Eph. 1:4).

The holiness of God is the heart and soul of his eternal mystery. Some of it is revealed in creation and history. After Adam and Eve fell into sin, God manifested his holiness by revealing and giving his name in order to restore man to the image of his Creator (see CCC 2809). He revealed his name to Moses in the mystery of the burning bush as "I am who am," I am the Lord.

Finally, in Jesus the name of the Holy God is revealed and given to us in the flesh, as Savior and Lord; it is revealed by what he is, by his word, and by his sacrifice on the cross on Calvary. In his resurrection the Father gives him the name that is above all names, "Jesus Christ is Lord, to the glory of God the Father" (Phil. 2:9–11; CCC 2812). There is spiritual power and salvation in the name of Jesus as St. Luke says in Acts 4:12: "And there is salvation in no one else, for there is no other name under heaven given among men by which we must be saved."

Our Father calls us to holiness in the whole of our life, and since "He is the source of your life in Christ Jesus, whom God made our wisdom, our righteousness and sanctification" (1 Cor. 1:30), both his glory and our life depend on the hallowing of his name in us and by us (see CCC 2813). This is a positive statement of the second of the Ten Commandments: "You shall not take the name of the Lord your God in vain" (Exod. 20:7).

The sanctification of his name among the nations depends inseparably on our life and our prayer. We must pray in imitation of Jesus and our life must be a witness to the reality of our faith. In this regard, Tertullian said: "When we say 'hallowed be thy name,' we asks that it should be hallowed in us, who are in him; but also in others whom God's grace still awaits, that we may obey the precept that obliges us to pray for everyone, even our enemies. That is why we do not say expressly 'hallowed be thy name *in us*,' for we ask that it be so in all men" (see CCC 2814).

In a certain sense, this first petition embraces all the others. Like the six petitions that follow, it is fulfilled in a perfect way by the prayer of Jesus as found in the Gospels, especially in John 17.

When we pray that God's holy name be sanctified, we pray that our minds, our souls and our lips may be so devoted to the honor and worship of God as to glorify him with all veneration both interior and exterior.

Also, as the angels with perfect unanimity exalt and glorify God, so do we pray that the same be done over all the earth; that all nations may come to know, worship and reverence God; that all may embrace the Christian religion and devote themselves completely to the service of God (see *Catechism of the Council of Trent*, Part IV, First Petition).

We pray for sinners and all who have abandoned their faith. We pray that in these also his name may be sanctified; that they may reenter into themselves and, returning to the right frame of mind, may recover their former holiness through the sacrament of Penance, and become once more the pure and holy temple and dwelling place of God.

With this first petition, we also pray that God may make his light to shine on the minds of all to enable them to see that "every good gift and every perfect gift comes from the Father of lights" (James 1:17), that all goods, both natural and supernatural, must be recognized as gifts proceeding from him. We ask in this petition that all may acknowledge and revere the spouse of Jesus Christ, our holy mother the Church, in which alone is to be found the inexhaustible fountain of grace that wipes out all the stains of sin, and from which are drawn the sacraments of salvation and sanctification which are like channels of divine grace flowing to us.

As faithful Catholics we should lead our lives in accordance with the doctrinal and moral teachings of the Church. When we do that we offer others a strong motive to praise and glorify the name of our heavenly Father. We should inspire others to honor God's holy name by the example we give of a virtuous life. Jesus tells us in the Gospel: "Let your light so shine before men, that they may see your good works and give glory to your Father who is in heaven" (Matt. 5:16).

Our Father, who art in heaven, hallowed be thy name. Amen.

OUR FATHER 2 – THY KINGDOM

Thy kingdom come

The second petition of the Our Father is "Thy kingdom come" which is directed to the glory of God. Here we are asking that God's rule over the hearts of men may become a reality. St. Mark tells us that, when Jesus began to preach in Galilee, the first thing he said was: "The time is fulfilled, and the kingdom of God is at hand; repent, and believe in the gospel" (1:15).

Since the resurrection of Jesus, the kingdom has been in our midst in a beginning and humble way in the form of the Church. It is a reality that grows and spreads. This is emphasized by Jesus in the parables of the mustard seed, the sower, the wheat and the weeds, the big catch of fish. The full flowering of the kingdom will take place at the end of the world when Jesus comes again in glory to judge the living and the dead. Since Pentecost the coming and growth of the kingdom is the work of the Holy Spirit who has been poured out on the Church by the glorified Jesus.

In the Sermon on the Mount in which he points out to his disciples the way to true happiness, Jesus begins with the kingdom of heaven: "Blessed are the poor in spirit, for theirs is the kingdom of heaven" (Matt. 5:3). He commanded his Apostles to preach the kingdom and after his resurrection, during the forty days when he appeared to them, he spoke of the kingdom of God (Acts 1:3).

The kingdom of God is righteousness and peace and joy in the Holy Spirit (Rom. 14:17). It means being a friend of God and living a life animated with the theological virtues of faith, hope and charity. Christians have to distinguish between the growth of the kingdom of God and the progress of the culture and the technological society in which they live. They are not the same. Increased control of the material environment by science and technology is not the same thing as the spiritual growth of the kingdom of God. The kingdom of God grows where faith, hope and charity grow and man recognizes, both individually and as a society, the majesty of God and submits himself to him humbly in the obedience of faith. It is both interior and exterior, but the most important dimension of the kingdom is the interior reign of the love of God in the hearts of men. Everything else flows from that.

Seeking God's kingdom should be the main goal of our life. If we strive to make the kingdom a reality in our life, our life will be a success on God's terms, not the terms of this world. Jesus himself said, "Seek first the kingdom of God and his justice, and all these things shall be added to you" (Matt. 6:33).

So great and so abundant are the heavenly gifts contained in this petition, that it includes all things necessary for soul and body. All that we need in our present pilgrimage towards God is contained in this petition, for Jesus says to us "all these things shall be added to you." Of course, in order to make the kingdom a reality in our lives we must use the means to reach it that God has given us—prayer, the Sacraments, especially Mass and Holy Communion at least every week, a life of virtue, and following the teaching of the Church.

The kingdom of God can be understood in different ways. It includes God's power over the whole universe and his providence which rules and governs all things. The prophet says in Psalms 95:4, "In his hand are the depths of the earth; the heights of the mountains are his also. The sea is his for he made it; for his hands formed the dry land."

By the kingdom of God is also understood that special providence by which God protects and watches over pious and holy men. King David speaks of this when he says, "The Lord is my shepherd; I shall not want" (Ps. 23:1).

Christ the King rules over a kingdom of justice, as St. Paul says in Romans 14:17, "The kingdom of God does not mean food and drink but righteousness and peace and joy in the Holy Spirit." As I said above, Christ reigns in us by the interior virtues of faith, hope and charity. By these virtues we are made members of his kingdom and are consecrated to his worship and adoration, so that St. Paul could say, "It is no longer I who live, but Christ who lives in me" (Gal. 2:20).

By the words "kingdom of God" is also meant that kingdom of his glory, of which Christ our Lord says in St. Matthew, "Come, O blessed of my Father, inherit the kingdom prepared for you from the foundation of the world" (25:34). This is the kingdom the good thief begged for when he asked our Lord on the cross, "'Jesus, remember me when you come in your kingly power.' And he said to him, 'Truly I say to you, today you will be with me in Paradise'" (Luke 23:42).

In this petition we ask God that the kingdom of Christ, now in its beginning stages in the Church, may be enlarged; that Jews and infidels may embrace the faith of Christ and the knowledge of the true God; that heretics and schismatics may return to soundness of mind, and to the communion of the Church of God which they have deserted; these and other petitions are included in the special prayers of the Church on Good Friday.

Finally, we pray that God alone may reign within us; that death may no longer exist, but may be absorbed in the victory achieved by Christ our Lord who, by his resurrection, has triumphed over death and Satan. Here we might profitably reflect on the words of our Lord: "The kingdom of heaven is like a treasure hidden in a field, which a man found and covered up; then in his joy he goes and sells all that he has and buys that field" (Matt. 13:44). He who knows the value of the kingdom will despise all material things in comparison with it. This is the precious jewel of the Gospel, and he who sells all his earthly goods to purchase it shall enjoy an eternity of bliss. That kingdom is much greater than anything we can imagine. As St. Paul says, "Eye has not seen, nor ear heard, neither has it entered into the heart of man, what things God has prepared for those who love him" (1 Cor. 2:9).

In order to enter God's kingdom and stay there we must exert ourselves. For we are not called to lead lives of ease and luxury. Jesus said, "If thou wilt enter into life, keep the commandments" (Matt. 19:17). We must cooperate with the grace of God in pursuing the path that leads to heaven. God never abandons us; he has promised to be with us at all times; he is more eager to help us than we are to receive his help. At the end of St. Matthew's

Gospel Jesus says, "Behold, I am with you all days, even until the end of time" (Matt. 28:20).

"Our Father, who art in heaven, hallowed be thy name; thy Kingdom come" into our hearts and into the hearts of all who hear your word and do your will.

OUR FATHER 3 – THY
WILL BE DONE

Thy will be done on earth as it is in heaven

The third petition of the "Our Father" is: "Thy will be done on earth as it is in heaven." This is a prayer or request that God's eternal plan of creation, redemption and sanctification be carried out everywhere. We all know what "will" is because we exercise it constantly during each day. Will is the desire for some known good; it is always moved by what is good or what appears to be good. No one desires evil for its own sake. When someone desires to do something evil, like theft or adultery, it is always done for the good that is seen in it.

God created each one of us and destined us for eternal happiness with him in heaven. St. Paul says that our Father "desires all men to be saved and to come to the knowledge of the truth" (1 Tim. 2:4). The only way to achieve eternal salvation is by doing the will of God. In the "Our Father" we ask for that for ourselves and for all of creation on earth and in heaven—what is visible and what is invisible. It is not a matter of words, but of deeds. Doing the will of God is the key thing. Jesus said in this regard: "Not everyone that says to me, Lord, Lord, shall enter into the kingdom of heaven; but he that does the will of my Father who is in heaven, he shall enter into the kingdom of heaven" (Matt. 7:21). Today almost all of those who believe in God want to go to heaven, but many follow their own will that is contrary to the will of God. Our Lord says that if they do not enter by the narrow gate and follow the hard road, they will not attain heaven.

Over the years as a Jesuit I have read many lives of the saints. One thing that stands out in all of them, whether martyrs or confessors or virgins, is that all of them sought to do the will of God in their life. That will is made known to us in the Bible, in the Ten Commandments, in the teaching of the Catholic Church, and in the particular circumstances of life that each one finds himself in.

Sometimes, however, it is very difficult to discover what God's will is in a particular situation, such as choosing a vocation in life, choosing a spouse in marriage, knowing what kind of treatment to give to a loved one who is dying from cancer. In such situations one must turn to prayer and seek light and inspiration from God on which course to choose. It can also be helpful to consult a wise person and seek his or her advice on what should be done.

The best example we have of doing the will of God is our Lord and Savior, Jesus Christ. His coming into the world, his life, death and resurrection were all done in accordance with the will of God. Jesus said on entering into this world, "I have come to do your will, O God" (Heb. 10:7). He also said, "I always do what is pleasing to him" (John 8:29). In his agony in the garden of Gethsemane, he uttered those words that we should all use in time of trial, "Not my will, but thine be done" (Luke 22:42).

There is a close connection between the second and the third petitions, for when we pray for the coming of the kingdom the way to achieve it is by doing the will of the Father, manifested to us by revelation and by the situation of life we find ourselves in. This petition is very necessary because of our inclination to follow our own will and to act against the will of God. This is one of the consequences of Original Sin and is called in Catholic theology "concupiscence." Concupiscence means a tendency in us towards evil. We have all experienced it. We all have to strive against the Seven Capital Sins: pride, avarice, anger, envy, lust, gluttony and sloth. At one time or another we are all tempted in one or more of these ways—feelings of pride, envy, lust; eating or drinking too much; rashly judging others; gossip; impatience, and so forth. In several places in his letters St. Paul gives a list of the sins that were common among the pagans in the Roman Empire. It is not a pretty picture of frequent human activity. All of these words and deeds are contrary to the will of God, so when we pray "thy will be done" we are asking that these sins be avoided.

A problem in the fulfilling of God's will is the weakness of the human will. In order to avoid sin, that is, to do the will of the Father, we need the help of divine grace. The main ways of attaining that help is by prayer and the Sacraments, especially frequent confession and communion. Continually beset as we are by interior and exterior temptations, it is not hard for us to understand that we must ask for God's helping grace so that we may overcome them and his will may be done in us.

There are many aspects of the will of God. There is, for example, his permissive will which means that he allows evil to take place for a higher good, namely the existence of free will in men and angels. But the primary emphasis in this petition, "thy will be done," is on his positive will, that is, we pray that whatever God has commanded us to do or to avoid will be carried out.

When we pray "thy will be done" we are asking our heavenly Father to give us the strength to obey his commandments and to do all things according to his will and pleasure. Whoever does the will of God is closely related to Jesus himself, for he says, "Whoever shall do the will of my Father in heaven, he is my brother and sister and mother" (Matt. 12:50). Also, when we pray "thy will be done" we are begging God not to allow us to give in to impure thoughts and desires, but to govern our weak will by his holy will. Finally, we pray that the whole world may receive knowledge of the will of God and that God's salvific will may be made known to all.

The angels and saints in heaven serve God happily and love him because of his infinite goodness and majesty. When we say "on earth as it is in heaven" we are asking for the grace of selfless love and obedience to God of all those on earth, especially the members of the Church, the Mystical body of Christ. The CCC on this phrase quotes St. Augustine saying it means, "in the Church as in our Lord Jesus Christ himself; or, in the Bride who has been betrothed, just as in the Bridegroom who has accomplished the will of the Father" (#2827).

No matter what happens to us, whether joys or sorrows, we must be convinced that none of these things can happen to us without the permission of God. We should say over and over again, "thy will be done." We should pray with Jesus "not my will but thine be done" and "into thy hands I commend my spirit."

In the Bible we have wonderful examples of submission to the will of God in Abraham, Moses, David, Jeremiah, Job, Joseph and Mary. This whole matter is beautifully expressed by Our Blessed Mother at the Annunciation. We should make her words and her interior attitude our own: "Behold the handmaid of the Lord; be it done unto me according to thy word." Amen.

OUR FATHER 4 – DAILY BREAD

Give us this day our daily bread

The "Our Father" has two main parts and there is a certain logical order between them. The first part deals with almighty God himself who is the Creator of the universe and everything in it. So the first three petitions refer to the glory of God, his infinite goodness and his providence. God is our first beginning and our last end. Because of his goodness he created us and destined us for eternal happiness with him in heaven. So in the first part of the "Our Father" we pray that those realities may be accomplished.

The second part of the "Our Father" is subordinate to the first part and has four petitions which concern man's earthly life—his bodily needs and his spiritual needs, since man is composed of both body and soul. Because of his goodness and love for man, God has concern for the whole man as we read in St. John's Gospel, "For God so loved the world that he gave his only Son, that whoever believes in him should not perish but have eternal life" (3:16). That love was revealed to us concretely in the life of Jesus who performed many miracles during his public life to cure the infirmities of body and soul of the blind and the lepers, and many other illnesses.

Today I want to offer a few reflections on the fourth petition in which we pray, "Give us this day our daily bread." Creation is good and man's life is good; both are willed by God. But in order to live a human life on this planet man has need of many things in order to survive. He needs food, water, clothing and housing among other things. These things are necessary for human life and so willed by God. In order to obtain these things a man must work, something natural to man, since even Adam was commanded to till in the Garden. But the hardship, sweat and monotony of work are one of the results of Original Sin, as we read in Genesis 3:19, "In the sweat of your face you shall eat bread till you return to the ground, for out of it you were taken; you are dust, and to dust you must return."

Man must work, yes, but it is God who makes things grow and his blessing is required for a fruitful harvest, as St. Paul says: "So neither he who plants nor he who waters is anything, but only God who gives the growth" (1 Cor. 3:7). Jesus tells us to ask for our daily bread in the "Our Father" and he promises to bestow it on us abundantly if we ask for it as we ought.

In the Bible the word "bread" signifies many things, especially the food and the other material things we need, and also the spiritual gifts of grace and the sacraments that he has given us for the salvation of the soul. When we ask for "our daily bread" we are asking for the things necessary for our daily sustenance, such as bread, meat, drink, clothing and whatever else we need to live a decent human life. Jesus, Mary and Joseph, the Holy Family, led a simple life but they had the necessities of life which they worked for and earned by the sweat of the brow. Thus they had sufficient resources to be able each year to travel the 85 miles to Jerusalem to celebrate the Passover and there is no indication that they were beggars in order to be able to do it. The word "bread" here does not include luxuries, but what is necessary and simple, as St. Paul wrote: "If we have food and clothing, with these we shall be content" (1 Tim. 6:8).

The word "our" here is very meaningful. The one praying is asking not just for himself, so he does not say "my" daily bread. By the "our" the one praying asks for a sufficiency of material goods for his whole family and for all mankind. Also, it is called "our" bread in the sense that it is to be acquired lawfully and by personal labor, not by any unjust dealings or by theft. For those who work honestly and hard, the Lord promises the blessings of success: "The Lord will command the blessing upon you in your barns, and in all that you undertake" (Deut. 28:8).

We ask for our "daily" bread. The word "daily" suggests moderation and is opposed to the desires of the greedy who want to accumulate immense wealth as a sort of protection against human mortality. We also call it our daily bread because we need food every day to renew our strength so we can pursue truth, goodness and contribute to the well being of others. Another reason for the word "daily" is to remind us each day that we are totally dependent on God and that we should worship him and thank him for the many benefits he has given us, especially the gift of life and the gift of faith in his Son, our Lord and Savior Jesus Christ.

When we say "give us" we are recognizing the infinite power of God who can either give or take away; we acknowledge that he is supreme in the world and that we are totally dependent on him. This is a prayer for both the poor and the rich. The poor need the basic necessities to survive; the rich ask God to protect them and that they may not lose their possessions. The rich are just as dependent on God for their health and welfare as are the poor. For if they make money into their god and final end, then they are spiritually dead and will end up in hell with Satan and those who are lost.

The "us" in the "give us" corresponds to the "our" which I just explained. Those who are blessed with an abundance of material goods are required to help others and to share them in a reasonable way with those in need.

The words "this day" remind us of our common weakness and they remind us that we should pray the "Our Father" every day. We have urgent needs each day so we ask our heavenly Father to watch over us and to take care of us day after day.

The word "bread" has a much broader meaning than just material bread and the other material necessities of life. It also includes our spiritual needs of the day, such as God's grace to be able to remain a living member of Christ's Mystical Body, the Church. The bread or food that nourishes the life of the spirit comes to us in several different ways. Of course the most obvious spiritual meaning is Holy Communion, which Jesus calls "the bread of life." The Fathers speak of it as "the medicine of immortality." We can also extend it to mean all the sacraments of the Church and the word of God which we find in the Bible and in the preaching of the Church. The word of God, like the Holy Eucharist, is our spiritual bread. In order to live a spiritual life we need the nourishment of that spiritual bread. Christ himself is that bread which is the food of the soul. As he said in John 6:41, "I am the living bread which came down from heaven."

The Eucharist is called our "daily" bread because the Mass is offered thousands of times daily throughout the world and is readily available every day for those who are properly disposed.

In all things we must be humble and subject to God. Whether we are poor or rich, when we ask God for our daily bread, it should always be in the sense of "thy will be done." God's primary concern is our eternal salvation. He grants and does not grant our requests according as the goods requested will contribute to our eternal salvation or not.

Today I have given you a few things to think about when you pray the "Our Father" and begin the second part by saying, "Give us this day our daily bread."

OUR FATHER 5 – FORGIVENESS

And forgive us our trespasses, as we forgive those who trespass against us

The fifth petition of the "Our Father" is: "And forgive us our trespasses, as we forgive those who trespass against us." The word "forgiveness" means the pardon or remission of an offense. An offense against almighty God is a sin and that is what the word "trespass" means in the English version of the "Our Father." Mortal sin means that a person offends God in a serious way by breaking one of the Ten Commandments and results in the loss of sanctifying grace. When that happens, the mortal sinner becomes an enemy of God and deserving of eternal damnation in hell. This is a perilous state to be in, and so the sinner should repent of his sin and beg for God's forgiveness. That God is willing and eager to forgive sins is clear from the whole Bible, from the sacraments of Baptism and Penance, and from the fact that Jesus taught us to ask for forgiveness in what is known as "the Lord's Prayer" or the "Our Father."

Jesus himself is a model of forgiveness. From the cross in the midst of his suffering he said, "Father, forgive them, for they know not what they do." He forgave Mary Magdalene who anointed his feet because she loved much. He forgave the woman taken in adultery (John 8:1–11). He forgave Peter who had denied him three times.

In the Lord's Prayer Jesus tells us to ask our heavenly Father for forgiveness, but there is a condition attached to it, for we ask to be forgiven "*as* we forgive those who trespass against us." We should all reflect on this for a few moments. Man is a social animal, so we are in constant contact with others in our family, in school, at work, at play and in the community in which we live. Because we are all limited beings, there are inevitable conflicts—sometimes we offend others and others offend us. There are enemies and friends.

In the secular society in which we live, a serious Catholic who lives his faith will encounter atheists and unbelievers who resent his faith; sometimes they will do or say things that are offensive and so they become enemies.

The dominant virtue of a true Christian is love—love of God and love of neighbor. Love in this sense means to wish well to others, even to enemies. On this point Jesus himself said to us, "Love your enemies and pray for those who persecute you, so that you may be sons of your Father who is in heaven; for he makes his sun rise on the evil and on the good, and sends rain on the just and the unjust" (Matt. 5:44–45). Therefore, when we pray the "Our Father" we acknowledge our sinfulness and ask for forgiveness just as we forgive those who have offended us. This is serious matter: if we do not forgive those who have offended us, then God will not forgive us. You should think about that and ask yourself if you have hatred in your heart for someone who has offended you and you have not forgiven him or her. If that is the case, then you have a problem in praying the "Our Father."

In St. Matthew's Gospel, right after giving us the "Our Father" prayer, Jesus adds this warning: "For if you forgive men their trespasses, your heavenly Father also will forgive you; but if you do not forgive men their trespasses, neither will your Father forgive your trespasses" (Matt. 6:14–15). It is significant that of the seven petitions in the "Our Father," the only one that Jesus explains further is this one about forgiveness.

In this petition we acknowledge our sins and ask for forgiveness. To do this properly we must have true sorrow for our sins and a purpose of amendment. We recognize that we are mere creatures who are totally dependent on God; he is our Creator who has loved us into existence, who has given us everything we have and we have offended him. Because of his infinite goodness, we know that he will forgive us if we ask him in the right way.

Also, please notice the plural. We pray "forgive *us our* trespasses." We do not pray, "forgive me my trespasses." Because of the Original Sin of Adam all men are sinners. So Jesus tells us to ask for forgiveness not only for our own personal sins, but also for the sins of others, for the sins of the whole world. This is an indication of the solidarity we have with others—we are all members of the one human family derived from Adam and Eve and all are either actual members of the Mystical Body of Christ or potential members. Forgiveness of sins means in a positive sense that the state of being an enemy of God is replaced with the state of being a friend of God, of possessing his grace and of being an adopted son of God. In the "Our Father" that is what we are asking the heavenly Father to grant. A sure sign that men are children of God is their willingness to forgive injuries and love their enemies. For in loving our enemies we resemble in some sense our heavenly Father who, by the death of his Son, reconciled the human race to himself and saved them from eternal damnation.

To make this petition fruitful we should avoid the near occasions of sin, be faithful in daily prayer, attend Mass regularly and receive Holy Communion often. We should think about those who prayed and obtained pardon from their sins. Such was the publican who, standing in shame and grief, with his eyes fixed on the ground, beat his breast and cried out, "O God, be merciful to me, a sinner" (Luke 18:13). Such was the sinful woman who, standing behind Jesus as he reclined at a meal, washed his feet, wiped them with her hair, and kissed them (see Luke 7:38). Finally, there is the example of St. Peter, the prince of the Apostles who, after denying Jesus, went out and wept bitterly (see Matt. 26:75).

Our heavenly Father is infinitely merciful and wants us to attain eternal life in heaven, but there are some conditions. He created us without asking us, but he will not save us without our free cooperation. He tells us to forgive those who have offended us, to love God with our whole heart and soul and our neighbor as ourselves. If we do that sincerely, we have a sure hope of obtaining life everlasting and the happiness we all desire. And so we pray, "Dear Lord, forgive us our trespasses, as we forgive those who trespass against us."

OUR FATHER 6 – TEMPTATION

And lead us not into temptation

The greatest enemy of our union with God and of our eternal happiness is mortal sin which makes us children of wrath and worthy of eternal damnation. In the fifth petition of the Our Father we beg God for forgiveness of our sins. We fall into sin because of some temptation. Thus, the sixth petition has to do with not giving in to temptation when we pray, "And lead us not into temptation."

In religious terms, what do we mean by temptation? Temptation is an invitation or solicitation to sin, either by persuasion or by offering some pleasure or other earthly advantage. There are three sources of temptation: the world, the flesh and the devil. Temptation from the world is the attractiveness of bad example, the desire to conform to others and to seek their approval. Temptations from the flesh are all of the carnal or spiritual urges of man's fallen nature that tend towards the seven capital sins. Pornography and human respect would be examples of this type of temptation. Demonic temptations come from the devil who encourages every form of avarice, lust or selfishness in order to lead us to pride and through pride to all other sins. We see this in the three temptations of Jesus in the wilderness.

Our Blessed Lord teaches us to offer this petition so that we may ask God daily for the grace to be protected from falling into temptation. Weak as we are, without his divine assistance we will soon fall into the snares of our crafty enemy, the devil. We should remember what Our Lord said to his disciples who were sleeping in the Garden of Gethsemane while he was undergoing his agony: "Watch and pray that you may not enter into temptation; the spirit indeed is willing, but the flesh is weak" (Matt. 26:41). What Jesus said to the disciples shortly before his death applies also to us: Watch and pray that you may not enter into temptation.

In this petition we ask God to give us the grace not to yield to temptation; that is the meaning of the words "lead us not into temptation." Here we are not asking to be free of all temptation, but only not to give in to it. The life of man on this earth is a spiritual battle between good and evil. We are all subject to temptations of many kinds from the world, the flesh and the devil. In the "Our Father" we pray for the grace not to succumb to temptation. No matter how pious a person may be, no matter how many Masses he or she may attend or how many Rosaries are said, there is no protection against temptations which can come from our own fallen human nature or from the world and the devil outside of us. No person, no place, no time is completely free of all temptations. We read in the lives of the saints that they were all tempted. Sometimes they fell and repented, like St. Peter, and sometimes they overcame the temptations, as St. Thérèse of Lisieux overcame temptations against faith during the last months of her life.

It is our responsibility to avoid the "near occasions of sin." That is a situation which we know from experience or instruction almost always leads one into mortal sin. If we deliberately put ourselves into a near occasion of sin, such as looking at pornography in a magazine or on the Internet, then we are in effect saying to ourselves that we want to do something we know is forbidden by God. That is what we mean by sin. When we do that we are rejecting God's grace and are leading ourselves into sin. We always remain free and God respects our freedom, so if we choose what is evil he will not prevent it. There is something very mysterious about this since it has to do with the relation between free will and God's grace.

God does not tempt anyone to evil. On this point St. James says, "Let no one say when he is tempted: 'I am tempted by God'; for God cannot be tempted with evil and he himself tempts no one; but each person is tempted when he is lured and enticed by his own desire" (1:13–14). God does not tempt to sin, but he does *try* individuals to test their virtue. There are many examples of this in the Bible. God tested Israel in the desert as Moses said in Deut. 13:3, "The Lord your God is testing you, to know whether you love the

Lord your God with all your heart and all your soul." He tested Joseph in Egypt who rejected the solicitations of a wicked woman (Gen. 39:7, 10, 12); he tested Susanna who was approached in her garden by the two wicked old men (Dan. 13:35); he tested Job who lost all of his worldly possessions but would not abandon God. We also see that St. Joseph, the husband of Mary, was tested when the angel made several strange demands of him and he always obeyed immediately with unhesitating faith.

In this petition we do not ask to be totally freed from all temptation, since human life is one long and continued temptation. Daily we encounter temptations to faith, hope and charity. But temptation helps us to grow in virtue, for it teaches us to know ourselves, to know our great weakness, and to humble ourselves under the mighty hand of God. St. James says, "Blessed is the man who endures trial, for when he has stood the test he will receive the crown of life which God has promised to those who love him" (1:12).

When we offer this petition in the "Our Father" we should remember our own weakness and distrust our own moral strength, while placing our trust in God and in his efficacious grace. Relying on him we can encounter the greatest dangers with undaunted courage and confidence.

In this regard we should recall the examples of Jesus, the saints, and many holy persons in the Bible. Jesus overcame the world and the devil, as he says to his disciples in John 16:33, "Have confidence: I have overcome the world." The Epistle of St. Paul to the Hebrews abounds with the victories of holy men who by faith conquered kingdoms and stopped the mouths of lions (Heb. 11:33). St. Paul, the Apostle, overcame tremendous obstacles in order to preach the Good News of Jesus Christ to the whole known world.

We are all subject to temptation, including the Pope, but we must have confidence that we can overcome it and grow in virtue. In order to triumph over temptation we must pray daily, receive the sacraments of the Church and avoid the near occasions of sin-whatever they may be. The rewards are great: union with God, the source of all goodness; peace of soul because of a good conscience; joy in the good things of life, and hope of everlasting happiness in heaven. Finally, the words of Jesus in the Book of Revelation are addressed to each one of us: "He who conquers, I will grant him to sit with me on my throne, as I myself conquered and sat down with my Father on his throne" (3:21)

Dear Lord, for all these reasons and more, lead us not into temptation.

OUR FATHER 7 – EVIL

But deliver us from evil

The seventh and last petition of the "Our Father" in a sense summarizes all the previous petitions: "But deliver us from evil." What is evil is injurious or destructive of our well-being either physically or spiritually. The human person, in this fallen world, is exposed to many kinds of evil that threaten him both in soul and in body. The evil referred to here directly is "the evil one," that is, the devil, Satan, who hates human beings redeemed by Christ and uses all his superior knowledge and deceit in order to entice man to disobey God and so sin, as he did with Adam and Eve in the Garden or Eden. Jesus teaches us in the "Our Father" to ask for deliverance from the deceits of the devil, and he himself prayed for his disciples and us in the same vein when he said to his Father, "I am not asking you to take them out of the world, but to protect them from the evil one" (John 17:15). Of all possible evils that can beset man, mortal sin is the worst, since it separates man from God who is the source of his being and is his final end in paradise.

If you reflect on it for a moment, you will understand that man is exposed to many evils every day. We all suffer something each day—either in the body or in the soul. It could be a headache or a stomach ache in the body, or being spoken to harshly, or feeling rejection by a relative or friend. Our Lord himself said, "Sufficient for the day is the evil thereof." So evil is something we experience each day. But when we pray to be delivered from evil we must always remember to do it for the glory of God. We cannot be delivered from all evils. In the "Our Father" Jesus is teaching us to pray to be delivered from those evils that are opposed to our eternal salvation in some way. Many people pray to win millions of dollars in the lottery, but God does not grant their wish because that amount of money might lead to their eternal damnation. So what appears to be good may turn out to be a great evil.

In all situations we must pray with confidence in God. He is infinitely good; he knows all things and he knows what is best for us. We ask to be delivered from the evil one because Jesus has commanded us in the "Our Father" to pray for that.

From what I have said so far, it should be clear that we do not ask for deliverance from every evil. That is impossible for a human being who comes into this world in pain and suffering and goes out of it in the same way when death approaches. We pray, therefore, to be delivered from those evils only which do not contribute to our spiritual well-being, not against those trials and tribulations that are profitable towards our salvation.

The meaning of this seventh petition, therefore, is that, having been freed from sin and from the danger of temptation, we may be delivered from internal and external evils; that we may be protected from fire, serious sickness, automobile accidents, a terrorist attack or whatever. We also pray that God will give us the grace not to fall into mortal sin. We beg of God that we not be taken by a sudden and unprepared death; that we not die without the grace of God; that we may avoid purgatory and go straight to heaven.

The goodness of God delivers us from evil in many different ways. If we are faithful in prayer and stay close to him, he protects us from possible evils. He protects us from the incursions of the devil. The devil is called the evil one because he is the author of the sin of Adam and Eve and also because God makes use of him as an instrument to chastise sinful and impious men. For many of the evils that mankind suffers God allows as a punishment for sin, as we see in the history of Israel in the Old Testament, for example, in the book of Judges and the prophets, especially Jeremiah.

In the Lord's Prayer we say deliver us *from evil* and not *from evils,* because the evil we experience from others really come from our arch- enemy, the devil, who is their author and instigator.

If our prayers to be delivered from some evil are not answered, we should endure it with patience, convinced that it is the will of God that we should so endure it. The idea behind the expression "God willing," which is so common in Irish spirituality, should always be present at least implicitly in all of our prayers for deliverance from evil. God knows what is best for us and if he does not answer our prayers the way we want him to, we should not feel resentful and bitter towards God. Whatever he does or allows to happen is for our own good, especially our spiritual good.

Again, human life is shot through with trials and tribulations. There is no escape, not even for the super-wealthy. In all things we need patience and perseverance, in imitation of Jesus and the saints. St. Paul wrote to Timothy, "All who want to live a godly life in Christ Jesus will be persecuted" (2 Tim. 3:12). And Jesus said after his glorious resurrection, "Ought not the Christ to have suffered these things, and so enter into his glory?" (Luke 24:26). Christ is our Leader and master and a servant should not be greater than his master. He also tells us to take up our cross daily and follow him (Luke 9:23).

In all of our trials, no matter where they come from, we should imitate the blessed Apostles who rejoiced that they were considered worthy to suffer beatings for Christ Jesus (Acts 5:40). So these are some of the reflections that we might consider when we pray, "But deliver us from evil."

We begin the Lord's Prayer by invoking "Our Father who art in heaven" and we conclude it by saying "Amen." "Amen" is a Hebrew word which means "so be it" or "truly." This word was frequently on the lips of Our Savior. Several times he introduced an important point by saying, "Amen, Amen I say to you...." This one word includes and repeats the seven petitions of the "Our Father" and by it we beg once again that our preceding petitions be granted.

We know that God is moved by the name of his Son, Jesus, and by the word "Amen" which was spoken so often by him who "was always heard for his reverence" (Heb. 5:7).

With this consideration of "Amen" we conclude our series of sermons on the "Our Father" and the *Catechism of the Catholic Church*.

BIBLIOGRAPHY

Aumann, Jordan, O.P., *Spiritual Theology* (Our Sunday Visitor, 1980).

Baker, Kenneth, S.J., *Fundamentals of Catholicism*, Three Volumes (Ignatius Press, 1982).

_____, *Inside the Bible. An Introduction to Each Book of the Bible* (Ignatius Ignatius Press, 1998).

Catechism of the Catholic Church (Libreria Editrice Vaticana, 1994).

Catechism of the Council of Trent (Roman Catholic Books, 2002).

Denzinger-Schömetzer, *Enchiridion Symbolorum* (Herder, 1965).

Flannery, Austin, O.P., *Vatican Council II. The Conciliar and Post Conciliar Documents* (Costello Publishing Co., 1981).

Gabriel of St. Mary Magdalen, O.C.D., *Divine Intimacy* (Tan Books and Publishers, Inc., 1996).

Hardon, John A., S.J., *Modern Catholic Dictionary* (Doubleday, 1980).

Ott, Ludwig, *Fundamentals of Catholic Dogma* (Tan Books and Publishers, Inc., 1974).